Value Chains Transformation and Transport Reconnection in Eurasia

This book focuses on the geo-economic and geopolitical impact of value chains transformation on the transport-logistic reintegration of continental Eurasian countries, with a specific focus on the members of the Eurasian Economic Union.

The author assesses the potential impact of current trends (global value chains fragmentation and decoupling) on Eurasian transport integration. The book combines in-depth analysis of the evolution of value chains and transport-logistics corridors across Eurasia with a geopolitical assessment of its implications for the EAEU's members' foreign and economic policy orientation. The author explores three key arguments: (1) the key to a successful and sustainable integration of the transport space of continental Eurasia is less the ongoing expansion of transcontinental transit and more the participation in intraregional and transregional cross-border value chains, even though this process is increasingly tied to the question of the geopolitical and geo-economic orientation of continental Eurasia; (2) even in a more regionalized world economy, the economic complementarities between continental Eurasia and the two manufacturing blocs at the edges of the supercontinent, Europe and Asia, represent the greatest chance for continental Eurasia for larger participation in high-value-added value chains; and (3) without diversifying trade and financial ties across Asia and normalizing relations with the EU, the combined effect of shifting value chains location across the continent and China's ambiguous and flexible transport politics might turn an unprecedented chance into risk, augmenting competition among and within countries which are members of the EAEU over traffic volume, FDI, value chain participation, and ultimately geopolitical and geo-economic dividends.

This book will be of interest to scholars and students of IR Theory, IPE, Geopolitics, and Regional Studies, as well as the related subfields of transport geography, economic geography, and logistics.

Jacopo Maria Pepe served until the end of 2020 as a research associate in the Global Issues Division at the German Institute for International and Security Affairs in Berlin, Germany. His areas of expertise include global and regional connectivity, transport, logistics, energy policy, value and supply chains, trade in Eurasia (including Eastern Europe and China), regional cooperation and alliances (EAEU, BRI), the Eastern partnership, and global governance/international order.

Innovations in International Affairs
Series Editor: Raffaele Marchetti, *LUISS Guido Carli, Italy*

Innovations in International Affairs aims to provide cutting-edge analyses of controversial trends in international affairs with the intent to innovate our understanding of global politics. Hosting mainstream as well as alternative stances, the series promotes both the re-assessment of traditional topics and the exploration of new aspects.

The series invites both engaged scholars and reflective practitioners, and is committed to bringing non-western voices into current debates.

Innovations in International Affairs is keen to consider new book proposals in the following key areas:

- **Innovative topics**: related to aspects that have remained marginal in scholarly and public debates
- **International crises**: related to the most urgent contemporary phenomena and how to interpret and tackle them
- **World perspectives**: related mostly to non-western points of view

Titles in this series include:

Trump and the Politics of Neo-Nationalism
The Christian Right and Secular Nationalism in America
Jeffrey Haynes

Russian Public Diplomacy
From USSR to the Russian Federation
Marina M. Lebedeva

International Perspectives on Public Administration
Henry T. Sardaryan

After Theory, Before Big Data
Thinking about Praxis, Politics and International Affairs
Friedrich Kratochwil

Value Chains Transformation and Transport Reconnection in Eurasia
Geo-economic and Geopolitical Implications
Jacopo Maria Pepe

For more information about this series, please visit: www.routledge.com/Innovations-in-International-Affairs/book-series/IIA

Value Chains Transformation and Transport Reconnection in Eurasia

Geo-economic and Geopolitical Implications

Jacopo Maria Pepe

LONDON AND NEW YORK

First published 2021
by Routledge
2 Park Square, Milton Park, Abingdon, Oxon OX14 4RN

and by Routledge
605 Third Avenue, New York, NY 10158

Routledge is an imprint of the Taylor & Francis Group, an informa business

© 2021 Jacopo Maria Pepe

The right of Jacopo Maria Pepe to be identified as author of this work has been asserted by him in accordance with sections 77 and 78 of the Copyright, Designs and Patents Act 1988.

All rights reserved. No part of this book may be reprinted or reproduced or utilised in any form or by any electronic, mechanical, or other means, now known or hereafter invented, including photocopying and recording, or in any information storage or retrieval system, without permission in writing from the publishers.

Trademark notice: Product or corporate names may be trademarks or registered trademarks, and are used only for identification and explanation without intent to infringe.

This book was originally conceived in collaboration with the Dialogue of Civilizations Research Institute, a dialogue platform bringing together diverse perspectives in a non-confrontational and constructive spirit. More about the DOC's work can be found at doc-research.org

British Library Cataloguing-in-Publication Data
A catalogue record for this book is available from the British Library

Library of Congress Cataloging-in-Publication Data
Names: Pepe, Jacopo Maria, 1984– author.
Title: Value chains transformation and transport reconnection in Eurasia : geo-economic and geopolitical implications / Jacopo Maria Pepe.
Description: Milton Park, Abindon, Oxon ; New York, NY : Routledge, 2021. | Series: Innovations in international affairs | Includes bibliographical references and index.
Identifiers: LCCN 2020055353 (print) | LCCN 2020055354 (ebook) | ISBN 9780367651664 (hardback) | ISBN 9781003131236 (ebook)
Subjects: LCSH: Eurasia—Economic conditions. | Business logistics—Eurasia. | Transportation and state—Eurasia.
Classification: LCC HC240 .P3795 2021 (print) | LCC HC240 (ebook) | DDC 388/.044095—dc23
LC record available at https://lccn.loc.gov/2020055353
LC ebook record available at https://lccn.loc.gov/2020055354

ISBN: 978-0-367-65166-4 (hbk)
ISBN: 978-0-367-67402-1 (pbk)
ISBN: 978-1-003-13123-6 (ebk)

Typeset in Times New Roman
by Apex CoVantage, LLC

Contents

List of figures and tables vii

Introduction 1

1 Transport integration and value chains in continental Eurasia: limits and potential 8

2 The 'continentalization' of value chains: an opportunity for Eurasia transport integration 15
  2.1 Europe's value chains 'go east': a new manufacturing core 15
  2.2 China's value chains 'go west': new inland production hubs 17

3 The impact on east–west transit corridors: between integration and competition 19
  3.1 The catalytic role of the BRI 19
  3.2 The Northern Corridor: routes via Russia or via Kazakhstan/Russia 24
  3.3 The Middle Corridor: the trans-Caspian route 28
  3.4 The Southern Corridor: the Iran–Turkey route 30

4 Deepening trade ties with Asia: the future of Eurasia transport integration? 34
  4.1 The rise of Eurasian-Asian trade 35
  4.2 The rise of Asia's FDI in continental Eurasia: first steps, future trend? 37
  4.3 Current limits and risks of Eurasia's transport integration in Asia's value and supply chains 40

5 COVID-19 and the evolving EU–China relation: game changer for Eurasia transport integration? 44
  5.1 COVID-19: a trend accelerator 44
  5.2 The EU between overreliance on China and strategic autonomy: back to Europe? 46
  5.3 China's adjustment to a changing reality: the BRI between 'dual circulation' and Asia's free trade agreement 48
  5.4 Implications for Eurasia's transport integration 52

Conclusion: geopolitical and geo-economic implications 56

References 61
Index 69

List of figures and tables

Figures

3.1	Number of Asia-Europe-Asia cargo train journeys, 2011–2017	20
3.2	Volumes transported in the Asia-Europe-Asia direction, 2011–2017, in TEU	21
3.3	BRI's east–west rail transport corridors	25
4.1	EU and China exports to broader Eurasia (including CIS, developing Asia, the Middle East, Iran, and Turkey), in billion US dollars, 2000–2017	35
4.2	Broader Eurasia (including CIS, developing Asia, the Middle East, Iran, and Turkey) exports to EU and China, in billion US dollars, 2000–2017	36

Tables

3.1	Cost for 20-foot and 40-foot containers along different overland and maritime routes	22
3.2	Existing and planned routes according to the China Railway Express Plan	27

Introduction

Geographically and historically, transport and trade have united Eurasia as much as geopolitical conflicts and imperial rivalries have kept it fragmented. The supercontinent has been criss-crossed by different, intersecting transport routes, which for centuries used to connect continental Eurasia[1] with the external powers and economic poles of Europe, Western Russia, Iran, Turkey, India, and further east, China. Interestingly, though, even during the golden age of transcontinental traffic, which – with ebbs and flows – lasted until the middle of the 14th century, no trader has ever travelled the entire route from Asia to Europe. In fact, no one needed to. One reason was that, although the logistics chain was complex and fragmented and the routes dangerous, well-established practice that had evolved over centuries optimized the reloading process at intermediate stations. A rudimentary but effective freight insurance system also provided some guarantees against thieves or loss of goods. The most important reason, however, was that Europe was not necessarily the final destination of goods; some trade volume consisted of non-finished goods often directed to immediate neighbours for final production before being re-exported. These activities constituted some of the first forms of cross-regional value chains, as in the trade of raw and processed silk between the Parthians, Kushan Empire, and Han Dynasty. Therefore, central and continental Eurasia simultaneously functioned as a transit space, final market, and production centre.

Throughout the past 500 years, a gradual geopolitical and geo-economic shift from the Eurasian 'ecumene' to the North European–North American space and from overland to seaborne trade has led to a sharp decline in the relevance of long-distance transcontinental overland trade and of these first rudimentary cross-regional value chains. During the 20th century, the Soviet Union sealed off this vast space from the rest of the continent – to the east, west, and south – and consequently limited its participation in the emerging globalization of value and supply chains. The collapse of the Soviet Union

2 Introduction

and China's economic rise suddenly reopened this large, largely landlocked region and seemed to offer unprecedented possibilities to reconnect with regional and global markets.

However, from the early 1990s until the outbreak of the global financial crisis in 2008, the impressive increase in cargo flows between Europe and Asia – and particularly between China and Europe (nearly €590b in 2019) (European Commission, 2020a) – has largely bypassed the space of continental Eurasia and scarcely affected overland transportation. Capitalizing on comparably low tariffs and large container vessels with a capacity of more than 20,000 TEU (20-foot equivalent unit), between 70% and 90% of Asia–Europe trade flows is transhipped by sea today. Consequently, projects to fully realize the transport potential of central Eurasian countries have long remained underfinanced, at both a national and a supranational level. This trend has limited the capacity of landlocked or semi-landlocked countries and regions (e.g., Central Asia, the Caucasus, Siberia, and the Russian Far East) to integrate into global supply and value chains and has made some of them prone to a monocultural, resource-based economy.

Without a doubt, oil and gas producers such as Russia, Kazakhstan, Azerbaijan, and, to a lesser extent, Uzbekistan and partially Turkmenistan, have profited by far the most from high oil prices and their active pipeline diplomacy. These factors have guaranteed a prolonged period of stability and growth. Many resource-rich post-Soviet countries have successfully integrated into the global energy markets and diversified their energy transport routes via active support for and participation in the construction of different pipelines. For its part, Russia has been able to strengthen its role as a major supplier of gas to Europe. In recent years, the country has also attempted to become a relevant supplier of oil and gas for the affluent markets of China and of the Asia Pacific via the Power of Siberia gas pipeline and the Eastern Siberia–Pacific Ocean oil pipeline.

The flipside of this development, however, has been the neglect of the non-oil sector of the economy and of non-energy-related transport and logistics infrastructure. This fact has made these countries and their national budget particularly vulnerable to external oil price shocks. Such an issue has become evident since the collapse in oil prices in 2008 and again in 2015, exposing the vulnerability of this economic model. The upcoming energy transition and the decarbonization of the energy systems will only augment this vulnerability.

Conversely, since the early 2000s and even more so since the 2008 financial crisis and the launch of the Belt and Road Initiative (BRI) in 2013, opportunities for a major diversification and modernization of the economies of continental Eurasia via transport and trade integration, at both a regional and a global level, have risen dramatically and have in fact never been greater.

First, the global spread of elongated global value chains (GVC), which accelerated since the early 2000s, has contributed to the emergence of the first tenuous forms of transcontinental supply chains across continental Eurasia. These result not only from a spatial 'dilution' of production networks from domestic to regional, continental and eventually global (Pomfret, 2020, p. 18) but first and foremost from a relocation of production agglomeration in the inland regions of two vast sub-regions on the edges of the Eurasian landmass (i.e., the European Union [EU] and China). In Europe, the EU eastern enlargement in 2004 accelerated the development of a regional production network centred on Germany; the supply and value chains of its companies, which include the Visegrad 4 (V4) countries, have gradually extended into Central-Eastern and Southeastern Europe to become Europe's new 'manufacturing core'. In China the launch of the Central and Western Development Strategy in 2004 marked the beginning of a government-supported and cost-induced territorial expansion of production activities toward central and western regions, more distant from the industrial districts of southern coastal regions.

As the industrial core of the two powerhouses at the edges of the continent has moved geographically closer, new technological innovations like digitalization of logistics and production have brought producers closer to consumers. Consequently, private and state-owned companies have also started linking their value chains in China to those in Central-Eastern Europe via overland corridors. And this happened long before the BRI was launched.

Second, at least since the outbreak of the 2008 financial and economic crisis, while the upward trend in Europe–Asia trade has continued – albeit more slowly – Eurasian (and Middle Eastern) energy producers have largely reoriented toward the affluent markets of developing Asia (Calder, 2011, 2018). For their part, Asia and China exports have slowly redirected toward developing Eurasian countries. This trend only accelerated on the eve of the 2008 economic and financial crisis. While the crisis hit Europe and the United States particularly hard, it forced China to approve an enormous stimulus package to foster infrastructure investment to compensate for short-term losses derived from the demand collapse in advanced economies. Subsequent overcapacity was redirected toward developing Eurasian countries, thus increasing Eurasian–Asian interdependencies that partially bypassed and decoupled from Western and European markets.

The 'continentalization' of economic activities at both ends of the continent and deepening Eurasian–Asian trade ties have hence suddenly reopened for the continental space a chance to profit from the potential spread of supply and value chains at the transregional level (Pepe, 2018). Consequently, since 2008 and especially since the oil price decline in 2013–2015, the political and economic elites of several continental Eurasian countries have expressed growing interest in a new, more diversified economic model that would take advantage of these transformations. Strategies for the development of the non-oil sector have been approved along with infrastructure development plans and an attempt to foster regional trade agreements and integration in transcontinental and transregional value chains.

While results remain scarce and unevenly distributed, the most visible of these attempts has been the creation of the Eurasian Custom Union in 2010, of a single economic space in 2012, and of the Eurasian Economic Union (EAEU) in 2015 among Russia, Kazakhstan, Belarus, and later Armenia and Kirgizstan. As part of the integration process, the upgrade and synchronization of all modes (land, sea, and air) of the transportation and logistics sector, as well as the creation of free economic zones, logistics hubs, and a coordinated industrial policy, have been rightly identified as the main instrument to accelerate economic diversification and cross-border market integration of the EAEU's member countries among themselves while establishing a transit space between Europe and Asia.

While transcontinental transit corridors have been successfully established, worsening Russian–European and nearly non-existent EU–EAEU relations have limited opportunities to further increase trade, financial, logistics, and technological ties with the EU, which are the major sources of investment and trade for continental Eurasia to date. Conversely, China's reorientation toward Eurasia and the launch of the BRI in 2013 has turned the country into a potential alternative source of investments and technology for continental Eurasia and Eurasian transport reconnection as an instrument for integration into the Asia-Pacific region.

Against this backdrop, a more sober analysis of the reality and perspective of the re-emerging east–west transport corridors at the transcontinental and transregional level (aside from 'Silk Road rhetoric') is essential to assess whether the countries of continental Eurasia – including members and non-members of the EAEU – can durably profit from this re-emerging network.

At the transcontinental level, while broader Eurasia as a whole coheres on land and by sea (Kaplan, 2017), overland rail corridors promise to garner a considerable share of freight revenues emanating from the Europe–Asia trade boom. However, transit revenues will not sufficiently realize the full economic potential of countries in the vast supercontinent, nor will these revenues automatically attract more foreign direct investment (FDI) to increase participation in emerging transcontinental value chains. Meanwhile, gains will not be equally distributed among the involved players;

economic and geopolitical competition among different corridors and players keen to enter a lucrative niche market will only increase, particularly because different routes will be uniquely influenced by the combined effects of technological, infrastructural, and financial bottlenecks, by the changing distance between production networks and consumers, and by China's ambiguous political and economic choices.

At the transregional level, a political and economic reorientation toward Asia supported by greater transportation and industrial links will not represent an alternative to Europe and the EU in the short term – nor will it allow for a balanced integration in the Asia Pacific, one which would prove equally beneficial for all Eurasian countries, primarily Russia and Central Asia.

To this picture is added the 2020 COVID-19 pandemic outbreak, which has exposed the vulnerability of elongated supply chains, thus accelerating trends toward re-regionalization of production, 'nearshoring', and reconfiguration of supply chains at macro-regional level which were already visible as a consequence of the US–Chinese geo-economic rivalry. European countries and the European Union have since then started questioning their overreliance on China's supply chains, pledging for a repatriation of production activities and a greater resilience and diversification of supply chains.

Conversely, China – under pressure both by Washington's decoupling policies and by the EU's growing scepticism – has started recalibrating the BRI as part of a general reassessment aimed at lessening dependencies on an increasing hostile geo-economic environment. According to the doctrine of the "dual economic circulation" included in China's 14th five-year plan, in the coming years China will recalibrate the structure of its economy, privileging domestic production, consumption, and local value chains. The country, however, will unlikely abandon the outward-looking policy of the past decades but rather increase the aggressive promotion of its technology and high-value-added products abroad and concentrate even more on controlling its own supply and value chains across Eurasia (Daryl and Sicong, 2020) and in Asia, as the finalization of the regional free trade agreement with the ASEAN (Association of Southeast Asian Nations) countries, Japan, Korea, Australia and New Zealand in November 2020 testifies.

These trends toward production re-regionalization, accelerated by COVID-19, will profoundly impact globally elongated supply and value chains, including those which have developed across continental Eurasia in the past two decades. They will hardly lead, however, to a wave of autarchic re-nationalization of production in Europe or China. While decoupling between the EU and China might prove impossible, the presumable outcome will be much more, a mix of 'nearshoring' attempts around existing production clusters in Asia and Europe and a diversification of supply and value chains toward developing markets across the Eurasian 'in-between' space, in the search for resilient, self-sufficient transregional production networks.

Consequently, continental Eurasia's transport integration will be confronted with increased competition between the two manufacturing poles in Europe and Asia over transregional value and supply chains and market access. The transregional dimension of Eurasia transport reintegration might consequently gain greater significance than the transcontinental one.

Against this backdrop, this book poses four major questions: what has driven the re-emergence of continental Eurasia as a potentially unified transport space? What are the main structural challenges faced by continental Eurasia when it comes to participation in international east–west transport corridors and in Asia's regional supply and value chains? Considering both current difficult relations with the EU, what are the geopolitical and geoeconomic implications that continental Eurasia, and specifically Russia, face when it comes to deepening trade and transport ties with China and the Asia Pacific? How will the COVID-19 pandemic presumably impact continental Eurasia's efforts to integrate in regional and continental value and supply chains and its relations with both China and the EU? This book is divided into five chapters: the first chapter focuses on the intraregional dimension, briefly considering the limits and potential of transport integration inside continental Eurasia along with the status of cross-regional trade and value chains inside the EAEU.

The second chapter focuses on the transcontinental dimension and discusses how geographic shifts in the production networks at the two edges of Eurasia, in Europe and China – which predated the launch of both the BRI and the EAEU – have triggered greater transport integration across continental Eurasia.

As rail transportation plays a crucial role in the economies of many landlocked countries in continental Eurasia, the third chapter explores the impact of value chain transformation and of the BRI on the establishment and rise of transcontinental east–west rail transport corridors. While stressing the positive effects of the BRI on transcontinental rail services and on greater transport harmonization across continental Eurasia, this part will also focus on how value chain relocation, China's evolving BRI plans, and technical and infrastructure bottlenecks might lead to greater competition among routes and eventually to further fragmentation of the Eurasian transport space.

The fourth chapter will revolve around the transregional dimension of Eurasia's transport integration, particularly in terms of the status, potential, and risks of Eurasia's ongoing reorientation toward China and the Asia Pacific as an alternative to Europe as a source of trade and FDI.

The fifth chapter will offer a first preliminary assessment of the possible combined effect of re-regionalization trends, decoupling attempts, and the COVID-19 pandemic on Eurasia's transport integration and transcontinental value chains, particularly against the backdrop of evolving EU–China economic and political relations.

The conclusion will present the main results and discuss the geopolitical and geo-economic implications for continental Eurasia, and specifically for Russia, as the major driving force beyond the transport reintegration of continental Eurasia.

Note

1 In this book, we generally refer to 'continental Eurasia' according to OECD's classification, which includes the following countries: Afghanistan, Armenia, Azerbaijan, Belarus, Georgia, Kazakhstan, Kyrgyzstan, Moldova, Mongolia, Russia, Tajikistan, Turkmenistan, Ukraine, and Uzbekistan. However, considering the geographic extension and diversity of this classification, we mainly refer to member countries of the Eurasian Economic Union, as this Union represents the most advanced attempt at institutionalized transport – economic integration on the continent. When discussing transcontinental transport corridors, we also refer to non-EAEU members, as well as to 'maritime' Eurasian countries such as Iran and Turkey, not included in the OECD definition. When discussing trade flows, we refer to a broader definition of Eurasia, which includes developing Asia and the Middle East. This choice is justified by the increasingly complex transregional transport, value chains, and trade linkages developing across the supercontinent, where the functional distinction in sub-regions has increasingly vanished.

1 Transport integration and value chains in continental Eurasia

Limits and potential

For the countries of continental Eurasia and their economies, transportation plays a pivotal role in the domestic development and for the integration into global markets. Generally, the roles of railways and roads vary by distance from a seaport or inland terminal, with roads generally preferred for distances up to 900 km and rail intermodal services limited to long distances from ports (more than 900 km). In the case of continental Eurasia, long distances from open seas, geographic extension, and scarce demographic distribution with a population largely concentrated in mid-sized cities scattered across a vast space have made rail transport essential. For instance, rail is the dominant mode of transport in Russia and the backbone of the country's economy: the rail sector generates 2.5% of the country's GDP and dominates freight transportation; its modal share, excluding pipelines, increased from 71% in 1992 to 85% in 2012 (European Bank for Reconstruction and Development, 2016). The same is true for many Central Asian landlocked countries.

After the dissolution of the Soviet Union, however, the Soviet unified rail network, which accounted for nearly 148,000 km of rails by 1991 (Westwood, 2002), was split into different national networks. The creation of independent republics in Central Asia and the Baltics created new border barriers to regional and global markets. With the end of the Soviet Union, the fragmentation of the integrated rail network proved critical: the Trans-Siberian rail line, the backbone of the Russian and Soviet internal transport network, lost direct overland access to southern, eastern, and southeastern markets as well as access to ports to reach Western European markets. Similar problems were faced by the new independent republics of Central Asia as well as of Eastern Europe: when landlocked or only having access to 'closed seas', dependence on the Russian rail and transport network created new asymmetric dependencies and coordination problems.

In fact, immediately after the end of the Soviet Union and the opening up of the former Soviet space, none of continental Eurasia's domestic rail networks were able to become a single functioning platform for transcontinental connectivity. The Russian rail (and road) network – as originally projected before the October Revolution – was extended greatly during the Soviet era and administrated as a unique entity by the Soviet Ministry of Railways. This huge infrastructure system, which encompassed 32 railways at the end of the Soviet Union, was jointly managed by the Gosplan, the Ministry of Railways, and local railways in cooperation with industrial clients. In this case, the railways of Central Asian countries were mainly used to ship bulk goods and raw materials to industrialized western regions and the European (Baltic) ports of the Soviet Union. After the dissolution of the integrated Soviet transport space, national companies in former Soviet states in Central Asia and the Caucasus assumed responsibility for newly created 'national' networks in the form of state-owned, integrated companies (mainly joint stock companies). The length of the transportation network they inherited varied between countries, resulting in diverse levels of complexity, maintenance requirements, and interlinked interdependencies. For example, Russia retained 3/5 of the system but lost the southern and western parts to Ukraine and the Baltic Railway Branch to the Baltic States. For Azerbaijan, the former Soviet portion became the national railway, while Georgia and Armenia had much more difficulty in dividing the rest of the Trans-Caucasian Railway among themselves. Uzbekistan inherited a large part of the Central Asian Railway minus a portion that became the Turkmen Railway. Kazakhstan inherited the longest railway network among the Central Asian and Caucasus states, including three branches: Alma-Ata, West Kazakhstan, and Virgin Land. A common element of all these new 'independent' networks, directly derived from the enduring orientation toward Moscow, has been (a) the dependence on Russian territory to link with global markets and (b) a lack of alternative routes. In the first years after independence, the network retained its north–south orientation and lacked direct east–west connections both domestically (e.g., in Kazakhstan, between Astana and Aktau) and in connecting with external countries. This problem lies at the core of present constraints, and new rail construction plans and lines developed before and after the launch of China's BRI have sought to address this issue. For example, the Kazakh rail network is mostly developed along the north–south axis in the eastern and western parts of the country and is particularly dense along the Russian–Kazakh border; until recently, however, it lacked a direct east–west line, passing through the central part of the country (Zhesgazan–Beineu). For a long time, the network also lacked border-crossing points to other countries. Often, there were no convenient routes to move from one place in a country to another, leading to several cases where rail lines linking two regions of a country must cross borders that had become international (e.g., between the Fergana Valley and other parts of Uzbekistan through Tajikistan; between the northern and southern Kyrgyz Republic through Uzbekistan, Tajikistan, and Kazakhstan; between northern and southern Tajikistan through Uzbekistan and even between two neighbouring regions of southwestern Tajikistan; and between several regions of northern Kazakhstan through Russia).

Accordingly, new dependencies emerged for Central Asian countries such as Tajikistan and Kirgizstan (until recently, tense relations with Uzbekistan had led to a transit blockade that essentially cut off Tajikistan from regional and global transport). In the case of Armenia or Kyrgyzstan, the inherited network was incomplete or even insufficient for connecting various regions within the country.

In comparison to Soviet times, the transport infrastructure network has lost its unitarity and functional interoperability while diminishing relatively quickly alongside an increase in economic activity since the early 2000s. Even when considering the transport network of the EAEU as a unified transport space (which it is not, thus far), with 1.6 million km of roads and 108,000 km of railways (Eurasian Economic Commission, 2014), the total length of the rail network is still less than in Soviet times. In general, the quality of infrastructure has been and remains a pertinent issue: while Russia's Trans-Siberian mainline is entirely electrified and double-tracked, the line requires modernization in its central and eastern sections to cope with the increase in cargo traffic and turnover. In other continental Eurasian countries, rail networks are only partially electrified and even fewer are double-tracked.

The development of a unified and functioning transport and logistics system has been traditionally linked to industrial policies, urbanization, industrial developments, and trade policy but also increasingly to participation in cross-border production networks. For example, in Soviet times, this unified transport and rail network proved instrumental to fostering industrialization and the creation of industrial and urban districts across the Union according to planners' internal but autarchic division of labour. However, efforts to industrialize continental regions like Siberia, the Far East, and Central Asia via greater transport connectivity failed in the long run. Central Asia and Siberia were integrated into the Soviet supply chains, mainly as producers and exporters of raw materials, to the more industrialized regions of western/southwestern Russia. A few countries, like Uzbekistan, were integrated as producers of manufactured products. Consequently, the transport and rail network of these regions better served the western Russian industrial complex than did the industrial diversification of these regions.

Following the end of the Soviet Union and more than 20 years of failed attempts at post-Soviet integration, the 2014–2015 creation of the EAEU between Russia, Kazakhstan, Belarus, and, later, Armenia and Kirgizstan represents a more serious attempt to institutionalize regional integration in continental Eurasia. This development also denotes an effort to take advantage of scale economies in terms of market size and production capacity in an era of increased regionalization and fragmentation of the world economic system.

In fact, the creation of the EAEU has paved the way to gradual, functional reintegration of the former Soviet transport network, which is nowhere near complete (Vinokurov, 2018). As opposed to the case of the Soviet unified transport network, this new integration attempt has not sought to centralize the control of infrastructure and assets but instead to synchronize cooperation among independent states and their national transport and network operators, in the context of market liberalization and development of modern services, as envisaged in the EAEU transport strategy (Eurasian Economic Commission, 2016). This attempt coincides with the idea of fostering a coordinated industrial policy to develop new cross-regional value chains while modernizing and diversifying the economies of country members. Within this scope, Article 92 of the treaty establishing the EAEU and Annex 27 to the treaty define industrial policy within the Union as being formed by member states with a focus on industrial cooperation and implemented with consultative support and coordination from the Eurasian Economic Commission (Eurasian Economic Union, 2014). In 2016, for example, Russia emended the rules on industrial assembly, particularly in the car industry, by decreasing the required percentages of local production in order to facilitate the establishment of cross-border assembly processes (Noerr, 2016).

To date, the EAEU-member transport network is the most extended of the post-Soviet space and the best functioning in terms of interoperability across continental Eurasia. This status is attributable to several factors: a similar gauge width (1520 mm), a common railway law, gradual tariff harmonization, and reforms to promote greater interoperability on the cross-border market for rail wagons and containers carried out since the establishment of the Union. If the rail networks of key non-EAEU members (e.g., Uzbekistan and Azerbaijan) will operatively be included in this emerging common transport market, then continental Eurasia's rail network can indeed become the backbone of greater economic development and cross-regional value chain integration.

However, the effects of increased transcontinental rail services on the economies of EAEU members and non-EAEU countries have fallen short of expectations thus far. Problems related to infrastructure (e.g., congested border-crossing points), rolling stock (lack of containers and rail cars, as in the case of Kazakhstan), traction (no privately owned or foreign locomotives have thus far been allowed to cross borders), and services (e.g., delays and corruption at border-crossing points and a lack of electrified freight briefs along some routes) have not been fully resolved. These issues continue to constrain functional integration in intraregional, high-value-added production networks. This pattern, along with a lack of free trade agreements with major manufacturing powerhouses, generates few incentives for foreign investors.

At first glance, mutual trade inside the Union and external trade have each increased since 2010, with the exception of the crisis years (2014–2016). Since 2016, external trade has even grown more rapidly than mutual trade, while mutual trade presents a more diversified structure (Eurasian Development Bank, 2019).

In this respect, stronger coordination of transport and logistics, both in terms of infrastructure modernization and in the elimination of non-trade barriers, appears fruitful and seems to support the economic integration process – even more so when considering that "cooperation in transport and logistics is regarded as one of the main depoliticized areas of integration that can really lead to economic goals set" (Pak, 2016, para. 6). For instance, the Eurasian Economic Commission has launched a massive institutional package to refine the Union's transport policy with a major focus on the harmonization of regulations and safety standards around all transport modes. At present, the highest level of harmonization has been reached in the rail sector with the creation of a single logistics company, the United Transport and Logistics Company–Eurasian Rail Alliance, by merging the assets of three national container operators: Belarus, Russia, and Kazakhstan. The company, launched in 2014, was reorganized in 2018 and 2019 (Belarus News, 2019a) to provide customers with better transport services across the single market, including harmonization of external rail tariffs and introduction of a single consignment note.

However, a closer look at the sectoral structure of mutual and external exports, both of which are critical when assessing the impact of transport network synchronization on participation in broader Eurasian value chains, presents a different picture. As the Eurasian Development Bank (2019) reported, mineral products topped the structure of mutual (23%) and external (55%) trade exports in 2018, reflecting the driving roles of materials and energy products in the Union's industrial production and trade relations. Conversely, manufacturing products play a somewhat more relevant role in mutual trade than they do in external trade. Machines, equipment, vehicles, and parts thereof constituted only 3% of total Union exports compared to more than 19% in the case of mutual trade (Eurasian Development Bank, 2019). The import share of machines, equipment, and their parts from third countries accounted for up to 45% of all imports, confirming the Union's dependence on capital-intensive, technological goods (Eurasian Development Bank, 2019).

The predominance of manufactured and manufacturing goods, including crucial intra-industrial goods, in mutual trade between EAEU members testifies that cross-border production networks among Union members are promising and emerging: already by the end of 2013, a year after the creation of the single economic space, there were more than 10,000 joint ventures in the EAEU with partners from EAEU member states (Ustyuzhanina, 2016). According to calculations, the three biggest manufacturing economies inside the Union – Belarus, Kazakhstan, and Russia, have a rather high potential for joint cooperation and for the creation of cross-border value chains inside the Union in a wide range of high-value-added manufacturing sectors with high diversification potential. These range from the transport sector (motor vehicles and parts, trucks, trailers, and railroad equipment) to the information and telecommunication sector (hardware manufacturing: computers, smartphones, and tablets, energy storage devices (batteries), integrated circuits), as well as to a wide range of strategic metal products (steel, aluminum, and copper, but also silicon, cobalt, zinc, manganese, tungsten, and niobium alloys) (Kofner, 2020a).

However, at the moment, such ventures are still limited to a few sectors (i.e., the nuclear power industry, automotive industry, space activities, and machine building for the military industry) and largely dominated by Russian FDI (Ustyuzhanina, 2016). Moreover, the scarce roles of manufacturing exports and high-value-added exports in total external exports and in the total export of finished goods (according to the Eurasian Development Bank [2019], only 29% of all exported finished goods in 2018 were high-value-added) suggests several trends: first, manufactured and manufacturing goods for intra-industrial trade are largely non-competitive on the global market; second, cross-regional value chains are scarce or relevant only at the intra-Union level; and third, integration in global or continental value chains beyond Union borders is still in its infancy, albeit with certain potential. Notably, a low level of exports of high-value-added finished goods, manufactured goods, and manufacturing intermediate goods (e.g., parts and components) in highly globalized sectors such as electronics, vehicles, and machinery equipment implies a low level of 'domestic content' in exports, which is critical to evaluate emerging economies' participation in global value chains.

Given the structure of mutual and external trade and the few economic complementarities among EAEU members, decreased transportation costs via better coordination and harmonization as well as upgraded infrastructure and logistics make particular sense if such efforts are considered functional to foster integration with the value chains of external manufacturing powerhouses in Europe and, increasingly, in Asia.

In this respect, current trends at the two edges of Eurasia offer an unprecedented opportunity for continental Eurasia: in Europe and especially in China, geographical shifts in value chains toward inland regions have paved the way for a pioneering and major transformation that could prove crucial to the sustainable transport and industrial integration of continental Eurasia in value-added production networks.

2 The 'continentalization' of value chains
An opportunity for Eurasia transport integration

2.1 Europe's value chains 'go east': a new manufacturing core

In Europe, following the EU's eastward expansion in 2004, a new manufacturing core in Central-Eastern Europe has emerged in sharp contrast to the historical, industrial 'Blue Banana' stretching from south England to the Italian northwest. This fact became even more apparent after the outbreak of the 2008 crisis, when different paths of economic growth emerged between Germany and some Central-Eastern European member states on one side and Western and Southern European member states on the other. There is a consensus on the fact that the distinct impacts of the economic crisis on different European economies – as well as the German resilience to the crisis – can be explained by, among other factors, the different levels of integration of single countries in the regional production cluster centred on German-export-oriented and globalized companies (Stehrer and Stöllinger, 2015).

According to the Vienna Institute for International Economics, there is increasing evidence for the emergence of a 'German–Central-Eastern European Manufacturing Core' (GCEMC), a joint geo-economic production platform with Germany (and part of Austria) at its centre, as a new production and export core of the EU. It has been argued that in the GCEMC, integration into the regional value chains of German companies and the trade openness that followed the EU's expansion in 2004 has helped the V4 maintain high manufacturing shares of GDP while giving Germany an unprecedented strategic advantage (Stehrer and Stöllinger, 2015). In fact, when examining bilateral aggregated data for imports and exports between Germany and the V4, as well as for the role of German FDI in the V4, one can find growing evidence for the emergence of a transregional production cluster between Germany and the V4 countries on its eastern border based on intra-industrial, intermediate assembled goods and re-exported goods (e.g., cars, vehicle parts and components, electrical machinery, general machinery, and mechanical tools). As a result, the trade exchange between Germany and the V4 countries has reached nearly €250b, and the four Central-Eastern European members collectively represent Germany's most important trade partners (Pepe, 2017). Exports from Germany and the V4 also constituted in 2011, at the peak of the Euro crisis, 42% of the EU's external manufacturing exports (Stehrer and Stöllinger, 2015).

While this regional production network remains highly dependent on intra-European and intra-EU trade, external dependence from non-EU, global, and continental markets has increased even more dramatically, mainly thanks to China: in 2015, the level of Germany's cumulative exports to Asia, non-EU Europe, and non-Eurozone EU was already higher than the level of exports to Eurozone countries (Pepe, 2017). Meanwhile, trade with China increased to €200b in 2018 to make China Germany's most important trade partner (German Federal Statistics Office, 2019), with trade largely concentrated on industrial machinery, vehicles and parts, and electronic equipment (Pepe, 2017).

China's demand for German final and capital goods (particularly cars, industrial machinery, and, increasingly, consumer goods), despite growing more slowly and suffering under the effects of the current trade war and transformation of the automotive industry, has proven resilient and robust. China's automotive market is the largest and fastest-growing automotive market in the world; the country's demand for capital industrial goods from Germany remains high, with China being the second largest market for Germany's industrial machinery (Verband Deutscher Maschinen-und Anlagenbau, 2018).

China's high demand for German goods and the country's integration into Germany's supply and value chains has had two direct consequences for continental Eurasia's transport reintegration. First, it reinforced Germany's – and indirectly, Central-Eastern Europe's – dependence on the vast Chinese market. As the EU's high share in Central-Eastern European external trade is largely a result of the V4's high intra-industrial trade (backward integration) with Germany, the V4's participation in the GCEMC increases their dependence on German–Chinese trade. Meanwhile, the geographic location, which is more insulated from the traditional northwestern European ports of Antwerp and Rotterdam, has made this space accessible overland across Eurasia as well as via intermodal routes through more southerly corridors or the Suez Canal, as we shall see later in this study.

Second, as the GCEMC has emerged as the new productive core of the EU and has grown disproportionately dependent on trade with China, German companies and German logistics providers have sought to expand their value chains across the continent to integrate regional value chains in

Eastern Europe with their production networks inside China at a time when just-in-time production and the spread of e-commerce and digitalized production are essential to decreasing transportation and warehouse costs. As Pomfret (2018, para. 16) wrote,

> As the [global value chain] phenomenon has flourished, value chains are becoming longer and more complex. Following from sub-regional zones such as Sijori or the Pearl River Delta in the 1980s and 1990s to 'Factory Asia' in the 2000s (*and Eastern Europe,* Author's note) the next step is to link the regional value chains of East Asia and Europe.

2.2 China's value chains 'go west': new inland production hubs

In fact, the development on the western edge of the Eurasian supercontinent might have had only a scarce impact on continental Eurasia's transport integration if a similarly major transformation had not taken place inside China at nearly the same time as the EU's eastern enlargement. In 2004, long before the BRI was launched, the Chinese government announced its Central Development Strategy with the aim of giving new impetus to the development of the central and internal provinces while decreasing regional imbalances with coastal regions that profited most from the reform process initiated by Deng.

Throughout the past 15 years, a mix of market-determined changes (e.g., rises in labour [German Chamber of Commerce in China, 2018][1] and land costs [Chang et al., 2013], particularly in coastal regions) and governmental–administrative policies has led to massive production relocation and industrial agglomeration ('clusterization') in central provinces.

As a result, new manufacturing production hubs centred on an array of value-added manufacturing industries, from automotive to electronics to petrochemicals, AI, and robotics, have emerged. These are largely concentrated around new urban, regional, and cross-regional industrial clusters, far from the southeastern coastal regions but closer to continental Eurasia. Among them, the Chengdu–Chongqing Economic Zone, the city cluster of Zhongyuan in western and central China, and the special economic zones in Kashgar, Horgos, and Urumqi in Xinjiang represent new growth poles inside the country, experiencing consistently above-average growth for a decade. While this trend could revert due to external and internal pressures, as of today many central Chinese provinces appear to be brushing off the economic uncertainty invading much of the country, with some growing even faster than before (Koty, 2019).

18 The 'continentalization' of value chains

The expansion of export-oriented inland industrial capacities and rapidly growing urban agglomeration in these provinces have led to increased demand for improved transportation and logistics chains. As a result, government spending has largely been concentrated on infrastructure, enabling massive development of the road and (high-speed) rail network necessary to connect these centres with the coasts as well as with the rest of the continent (Pepe, 2018, pp. 282–328). As Wan and Liu (2009, p. 7) explained, when the effects of the two strategies had yet to bear fruit, "the logistics chains of export-oriented trade [were] extending ever further inland and logistics channels [were] required to bridge the structural discrepancy between coastal and inland economies."

Meanwhile, the strong integration of the Chinese export-oriented economy into global markets has led to growing congestion of its own ports, hinterland connections to ports, and the need to upgrade and diversify the transport network and increase the intermodal capacity of the country across Eurasia, creating alternatives to southern Chinese ports. As such, the combined effect of emerging new industrial clusters and export-oriented industries in inland regions and the need to bypass inland bottlenecks and avoid long shipping times has greatly contributed to the development of alternative and faster supply chains and overland logistics solutions across Eurasia. Therefore, the industrial and urban clusters of Chongqing, Chengdu, and Zhongyuan have emerged not only as the most important industrial and economic zones in western and central China, but also as logistics and transportation hubs for transcontinental traffic to and from China across continental Eurasia to the new Central European manufacturing core.

Note

1 According to a study by *The Beijing Axis* (2014), which refers to National Bureau of Statistics data, average annual wages for urban workers in China rose by 17.4% between 2002 and 2012. This trend continued throughout 2012–2018, albeit at a slower pace, with average wage growth of about 10%–12%, with coastal provinces experiencing the second-highest wage increase while exhibiting the highest salary level in the country.

3 The impact on east–west transit corridors
Between integration and competition

3.1 The catalytic role of the BRI

Structural transformations in value chains' location – beyond and before China's BRI – have surely made possible the development of east–west rail connections. By bringing production networks with producers and consumers at the two edges of the supercontinent closer, delivery time has been reduced for certain types of value-added consumer and capital goods. Overland alternatives to the sea routes connecting southeast Chinese and northwestern European ports have also opened.

In fact, Asia–Europe rail cargo transport started with a single trial in 2008, when the first train was sent from Hamburg to Shanghai via German railway company Deutsche Bahn upon request of the American computer producer HP to find a cheaper solution for rerouting computer and electronic parts from China to Europe. However, given that a long-distance overland rail service connecting two ports as destinations makes less economic sense, this approach was a one-time experiment to test feasibility, costs, and infrastructure constraints along the route.

It was only in 2011 that Asia–Europe rail cargo services started on a more regular basis, with 17 trains dispatched from China's inland city region of Chongqing to Europe's inland distribution hubs in Poland and Germany (Duisburg).

At that time, before the BRI was announced, demand for these services came mainly from private companies interested in quicker just-in-time delivery solutions to connect their value chains in Asia and Europe, particularly after the relocation of production activities in central China. For example, German companies like VW, Porsche, and Bosch, which had production plants in Central-Eastern Europe and central China, opted for this solution.

This being said, the BRI, along with the establishment of the EAEU single economic and custom space, has played a crucial, catalytic role in the

20 *The impact on east–west transit corridors*

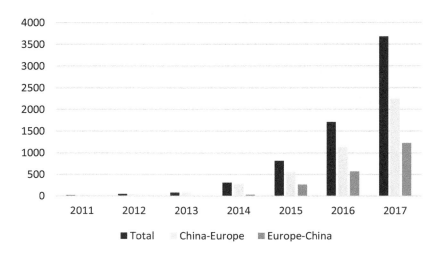

Figure 3.1 Number of Asia-Europe-Asia cargo train journeys, 2011–2017
Source: China Railways data; author's own graph

sudden increase of transcontinental rail services. Facilitated by political and financial support from the BRI, private companies and 3PL/4PL providers have become increasingly interested in these services, with the number of operated trains rocketing from less than 300 in 2014 to roughly 1,800 in 2016 and to nearly 3,700 in 2017, largely due to the combined effect of China's generous subsidization and simplified custom procedures in the EAEU. Transport volume grew from 3,000 TEU in 2011 to 145,000 TEU in 2016 and further increased to almost 420,000 TEU in 2017.

Today, in terms of value, roughly 7% of EU–China trade is transported by rail across Eurasia and, via Central-Eastern Europe, to the affluent markets of Western Europe. European and German companies producing in Central-Eastern Europe are increasingly using eastbound services to deliver parts and components for final goods to be assembled in China. This proportion represents a huge increase compared to less than 1% in 2012, allowing for an estimated trade value of $45b.[1]

While these increases in services and value are indeed impressive, volumes remain quite low when compared to those of maritime transport and will likely never be able to challenge long-distance seaborne trade. Asia–Europe volumes reached roughly 15 million TEU in 2017 (China–Europe: 10 million TEU) (Knowler, 2017), worth roughly €590 billion (European

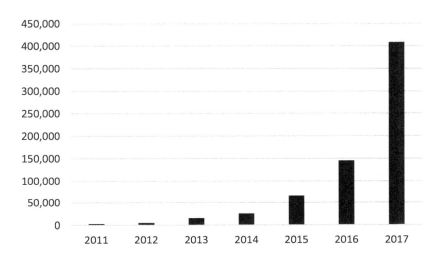

Figure 3.2 Volumes transported in the Asia-Europe-Asia direction, 2011–2017, in TEU

Source: Berger (2017); author's own graph

Commission, 2020a). More than 90% of this trade is still carried by ship using well-established sea trade lines via the Malacca Strait and the Suez Canal. The combined effect of low shipping rates and large vessels contributes to this.

Particularly, in terms of costs, rail services between China and Europe are well above those for maritime transport. As Table 3.1 shows, shipping rates for 40-foot containers (standard for maritime transport) range between $1,000 and $4,000 on the Shanghai–Rotterdam or Shanghai–Hamburg route, depending on market conditions and global demand.

In the first six months of 2019, the shipping rates on these routes sank to roughly $1,500 for a 40-foot container. On the contrary, rail transport rates for 20-foot containers in single-wagon loads on the Hamburg/Duisburg–Lanzhou route are nearly twice as expensive on average. A better transport cost ratio can generally be achieved by either (a) building block train services, which require a standard regular service from terminal to terminal (typically for the same client) but are less flexible or (b) shipping higher volumes, which would allow trains to be built with containers from different clients with the goal of commercial sustainability of all services. In Asia–Europe rail cargo transport, more balanced flows between eastbound

22 The impact on east–west transit corridors

Table 3.1 Cost for 20-foot and 40-foot containers along different overland and maritime routes

Route Duisburg/ Hamburg-Lahnzu/ Chonquing	40-foot container (full load)	20-foot container (full load)		Time (in days)
		Single wagon	Block train	
TransSib/ TransKazach	–	6,730 USD	3,300 USD	18–28 (possible: 10)
TransSib/ TransMongolian	–	6,705 USD	4,500 USD	20–22
TransKazach/ TransCasp	–	6,773 USD	–	15–20
Maritime	1,000–4,000 USD			45

Source: modified from Pepe (2018, p. 277); based on data from DB Schenker, KTZ, Retrack

and westbound trains would greatly contribute to this scope. As Figure 3.1 shows, there have been substantial improvements in this issue over the past couple of years, particularly thanks to German companies' increased interest in using the overland connection for just-in-time deliveries from their production plants in Central Europe. Operators like Deutsche Bahn already offer more flexible and customized solutions for different clients, who can now book a single delivery container on a regular train. However, the westbound-to-eastbound ratio was still relatively unbalanced in 2017.

Considering the high costs, one reason for the boom in Eurasia rail cargo lies in China's decision to generously subsidize these services as part of the BRI. According to an internal, non-publicly-disclosed source, these subsidies exceed $4,000 per TEU on the EU–China route and $1,500 from China to Russia and Eastern Europe (Knowler, 2018). Should either the central or local government stop subsidizing these services by 2021, the future of overland rail services will rely completely upon their capacity to stand up commercially (National Development and Reform Commission, 2016). In this sense, the initial effects of a step-by-step reduction in subsidies (now only granted to fully loaded westbound trains), as implemented during 2019, are already evident in a relative decline in rail service frequency. This indicates that in the future, the smaller the subsidies, the more traffic will be consolidated along fewer routes, with fewer operators and service providers presumably existing in the market; larger operators will likely concentrate on corridors that more rapidly connect industrial and consumer hubs in the continental production networks at the two ends of the continent (van Leijen, 2019).

The evolution of China's subsidy policy will massively influence two aspects that make transcontinental rail cargo transport solutions currently appealing: time and timeliness. Goods along all Eurasian overland corridors can be delivered in half the time (15–20 days) required for container ships to reach North European ports via the Suez Canal (45 days). Thus, rail solutions are particularly attractive for certain types of high-value, just-in-time goods like pharmaceuticals, automotive parts, electronics, white goods, and perishable/luxury goods. Rail transport therefore occupies a niche between cheap but slow maritime transport and fast but hugely expensive air freight (Rastogi and Arvis, 2014).

The second factor is timeliness (i.e., guaranteed delivery of goods on time, without delays and intact). Timeliness includes and is influenced by other important factors: the efficiency of customs and border management clearance; the quality of trade and transport infrastructure, particularly for developing countries; the ease of arranging competitively priced shipments; the competence and quality of logistics services; the ability to track and trace consignments; and the frequency with which shipments reach consignees within scheduled or expected delivery times (The World Bank, 2018a).

In the next two years, China – while decreasing subsidies and consolidating traffic – plans to further increase the level of Eurasian rail cargo services to 5,000 trips/yearly (National Development and Reform Commission, 2016). This intended volume also represents a further increase in terms of the value and freight revenue that countries en route can extract from transcontinental services.

From a more long-term perspective, a recent study from the OECD International Transport Forum concludes that even

> in a baseline scenario, international freight tonnage through Central Asia will increase over 60% by 2030 and 220% by 2050 from their 2015 levels. The trade flows between Europe and China will increase two times by 2030 and almost five times by 2050.
> (International Transport Forum, 2019, p. 47)

Against the backdrop of falling subsidies and consequential consolidation of traffic with a simultaneous expected increase in freight volume ('more traffic, fewer routes'), the development of efficient logistics services and supply chain management in continental Eurasia becomes a critical factor for assessing the competitiveness of single countries along routes that cross different territories and regulatory systems.

However, the combined effect of increasing traffic volume consolidated along fewer corridors and the need for rapid and reliable delivery (i.e., time and timeliness) will presumably increase competition among countries and routes across continental Eurasia (The World Bank, 2018b).[2] When taking time and timeliness as key factors, the competition among Eurasian corridors will eventually be decided by a mix of the following: distance from origin to final consumer/client; status of physical infrastructure; efficient supply and corridor management; and price competitiveness. This will, however, decisively affect how different continental Eurasian countries, including members of the EAEU, will compete or cooperate in the process of aligning different transport routes as well as their chances to integrate into the emerging continental value chain.

In the following paragraphs, considering the aforementioned factors as well as the relocation of economic activities, we will briefly assess the status and limits of the three existing overland east–west corridors crossing the territory of continental Eurasia along with how China's decision might affect Eurasia's transport reconnection.

3.2 The Northern Corridor: routes via Russia or via Kazakhstan/Russia

Currently, nearly all Eurasia container trains use the so-called Northern Route via Russia (Route 1 on the map) and/or the so-called New Eurasian Land Bridge via Kazakhstan and Russia (Route 2 on the map). The Northern Route via Russia is the oldest and runs the entire length of the Trans-Siberian rail line from the Polish–Belarusian border to northeastern China (via Manzhuli; 1a on the map) or to northern China via Mongolia (Trans-Mongolian route; 1b on the map). According to confidential sources, roughly half (around 1,800 between the two branches) of all Europe–China trains (3,663) passed along the Northern Route in 2017. The remaining half are routed through the New Eurasian Land Bridge, which is currently the single most-used route. It starts from the Pacific port of Lianyungang in China, traverses the mentioned industrial and urban centres of central-western China (Chengdu and Chongqing), and enters Kazakhstan at the two border-crossing points of Khorgos and Dostyk at the Kazakh–Chinese border before entering the Trans-Siberian rail line at Petropavlovsk station, further west.

Even though the New Eurasian Land Bridge came into operation relatively recently (between 2011 and 2013), both routes have equally well-established operations, high reliability in terms of delivery time, and good infrastructure. These two routes are also the fastest (see Figure 3.3), with potential delivery times between ten and 22 days. According to the World Bank (2018c), all countries involved in the Northern Route and the Eurasian Land Bridge improved their performance by several points between 2012 and 2018, with the notable exceptions of Poland and Belarus.

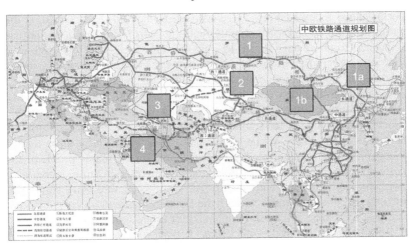

Figure 3.3 BRI's east–west rail transport corridors
Source: National Development and Reform Commission (2016, p. 5), modified by the author

These two routes are projected to remain the essential backbone of east–west cargo transport between Asia and Europe; even in the most conservative scenario, they will increase their capacity to 600,000–800,000 TEU by 2027 (Berger, 2017) compared to other more southerly alternatives, which we will discuss in the next sections.

However, both routes face two major challenges that could present opportunities for greater differentiation of services and corridors, thereby boosting other continental countries' chances to profit from trans-Eurasian transit. The first constraint is infrastructural; the second, which is more geo-economic, is related to the location of production and consumer markets and driven by China's evolving political and economic priorities.

In terms of infrastructure, given increasing volumes, bottlenecks at key transfer points can lead to significant delays, thus reducing the timeliness and attractiveness of the Northern Route and forcing freight forwarders and logistics operators to seek alternatives. While unloading procedures due to different gauge systems at the Kazakh–Chinese border have improved significantly and the unloading time has fallen below 47 minutes for a fully loaded container train, the transfer point at the Belarusian–Polish border (Belarus–Małaszewicze) presents the greatest bottleneck. The crossing point in Brest is included in almost all routes linking China and the EU and is hence the most intensive container train traffic node. Notably, Poland and Belarus are the only two countries along the two northern routes whose overall logistics performance index rankings have worsened since 2012. Since 2011, the travel time from Asia to Europe through the Polish–Belarusian border has improved from 25 days to 14–15 days but lags far behind the envisaged nine days. According to freight forward operators and logistics companies, this dysfunctionality is largely due to delays on the Polish side resulting from managerial, rather than infrastructural, problems (van Leijen, 2018). A study from the Eurasian Development Bank revealed that the Polish side processes only nine or ten trains per day instead of the negotiated 14 trains (Lobyrev et al., 2018). While managerial issues, particularly those related to dysfunctional custom clearance procedures, are a major problem, the current relatively poor state of Poland's railway infrastructure, locomotive fleet, and rolling stock undoubtedly adds to this picture. Any significant increase in container traffic through the Brest–Małaszewicze crossing point is thus bound to be extremely problematic (Lobyrev et al., 2018).

Against this backdrop, with China, Russia, and Kazakhstan all set to increase trains and volumes along the east–west direction and with Poland instead more willing to invest in north–south connections between the Baltic Sea and the Black Sea, the Polish–Belarusian bottleneck might prove crucial to reducing the mid- to long-term competitiveness of the Northern Route.

Furthermore, the Trans-Siberian rail line represents another infrastructure constrain: the Trans-Siberian line is already an overloaded artery, with transit capacity for containers limited to only 250,000 to 300,000 TEU. Modernization plans notwithstanding, a generally insufficient level of investment in the modernization of the eastern section of the Trans-Siberian rail line, which is especially crucial along the Northern Route, continues to limit the delivery speed and reduce the chance to effectively increase traffic turnover from Northern China via Mazhuli and Erenort in the short to medium term. The Northern Route is therefore increasingly dependent on the detour via Kazakhstan, which completely bypasses the eastern section of the Trans-Siberian line.

As for geo-economic constraints, the combined effect of China's new industrial and manufacturing hubs in central provinces and the strong concentration of production activities in Central-Eastern Europe (Pepe, 2017), along with sinking subsidies and China's evolving rail corridor plans (National Development and Reform Commission, 2016), have created incentives to seek alternative routes to connect with Europe and the Middle East via more southerly routes.

In 2016, China's National Reform and Development Commission released a five-year railway plan entitled 'China Railway Express 2016–2020' (National Development and Reform Commission, 2016). It proposed the rationalization, centralization, and coordination of rail freight services by consolidating traffic along three main corridors (Eastern, Central, and

Western, the latter of which is split into two branches through the Caspian Sea and Azerbaijan or through Iran; see Figure 3.3) defined according to the Chinese regions served by each corridor. The cities of Chongqing and Chengdu were among a group of internal cities set to become domestic consolidation hubs; traffic from the industrialized southern and central regions is collected and dispatched there. In this way, traffic could be concentrated and channelled across Eurasia through selected transhipment hubs at border-crossing points in the north, northwest, and west. As a result of this plan, Eurasian final destinations behind the EU/Europe have increased massively, particularly in Russia (six), Central Asia (seven), and the Middle East (four). Russia could consistently increase the number of services, adding six routes to the existing three, mostly for bilateral traffic.

By the end of 2020, however, Russia had fewer total bilateral services with China than had Kazakhstan. Moreover, only a few routes were added, which exclusively use the Manzhuli or Erenhot (Inner Mongolia) border-crossing points to Western Russia and Europe. Most are in direct competition with Horgos (Dostyk) for traffic out of China and Europe from respectively central-western China and Central-Southeastern Europe.

Table 3.2 Existing and planned routes according to the China Railway Express Plan

Operating: 23 routes from 23 cities

EU-Europe		Eurasia			
Western Europe	Central-Eastern Europe	Kazakhstan	Russia	Mongolia	Belarus
Spain: 1	Germany: 7 Poland: 2 Czech R.: 1	7	3	1	1
Total Existing: 12		Total Existing: 11			

Planned by 2020: 27 routes from 20 cities

EU-Europe		Eurasia					
Western Europe	Central-Eastern Europe	Kazakhstan	Russia	Mongolia	Belarus	Iran	Turkey
Netherlands: 1	Germany: 5 Poland: 1	6	6	3	1	3	1
Total Planned: 7 **Total (Ex+Pl): 19** Main Consolidation Hubs and BCP:		Total Planned: 21 **Total (Ex+Pl): 32** Dostyk/Horgos, Brest/Malashevice, Almaty, Teheran, Istanbul, Moscow, Duisburg					

Source: author's own creation based on data from National Development and Reform Commission, 'China Railway Express Plan 2016–2020', 2016

In particular, the Kazakh border-crossing point at Horgos and Dostyk will become the main transhipment hub from the industrialized regions of central, western, and southwestern China to new final destinations in Central Asia and the Middle East (National Development and Reform Commission, 2016). This shift in priorities from the Northern Route (Eastern and Central in Chinese nomenclature) to the Western route (Middle and Southern Corridor) and the rebalancing of traffic destinations from northern Europe to Central-Eastern and Southeastern Europe to access the new Central Eastern Manufacturing Core might pave the way to greater intra-Eurasian corridor competition, both between the Russian-only and Kazakh/Russian route as well as between them and other more southerly routes.

Within this context, even Russia, whose network has been primarily used by Asian shippers to transport cargo to Germany, Poland, and Bulgaria via the Northern Route to date, now has plans to attract at least a portion of Asian cargo intended for Southern European states, including cargo from China (Gerden, 2018). Russia's interest in increasing container volumes via the southern port of Novorossiysk as a detour from the Kazakh port of Aktau is clearly aimed at offsetting its geo-economic disadvantage vis-à-vis more southerly routes. In fact, both the so-called Southern Route via Iran and Turkey and the Middle Corridor through Azerbaijan, Georgia, and Turkey might have fairly good chances of attracting additional volumes or diverting freight from the Northern Route and the new Eurasian Land Bridge.

3.3 The Middle Corridor: the trans-Caspian route

Capitalizing on infrastructure bottlenecks along the Northern Route, the locations of new manufacturing clusters inside China and Europe, and Beijing's evolving rail corridor priorities, southerly corridors through central Eurasia – which only partially cross the territory of the EAEU – could clearly become important gateways and consolidation hubs, thus redirecting part of the traffic coming from central-western China across Central Asia and the Caspian Sea en route to Europe via the Middle Corridor (also known as the EU-sponsored Transport Corridor Europe–Caucasus–Asia [TRACECA]).

The Middle Corridor has two distinctive geo-economic and geostrategic advantages compared with the northern and the more southerly route, the Southern Corridor (to be discussed in the next paragraph): the Middle Corridor is the shortest route between China's industrial districts in the country's central and western provinces and the southern-eastern border of the EU (i.e., under ten days). It is also the most flexible, as traffic can be rerouted or consolidated along different alternative branches and ports, but is prone to greater competition. On the eastern shore of the Caspian Sea, traffic can be either collected at the Aktau port in Kazakhstan or at the Turkmenbashi port in Turkmenistan, while there are several options on the Black Sea: the Anaklia deep-sea port in Georgia (if completed) and the Constanta Port each represent an increasingly interesting multimodal option across the Black Sea; Novorossiysk could represent a further gateway on Russian territory. For its part, the Baku–Tiflis–Kars (BTK) railway offers new overland options for an uninterrupted rail link via Turkey to Istanbul and Europe. Against this backdrop, Azerbaijan is crucially located; the new Alyat port can profit from competition between Aktau and Turkmenbashi, while the new BTK can profit from competition between the multimodal route across the Black Sea and the overland route across Turkey. In terms of infrastructure and logistical development along the corridor, 2017 represented a turning point after years of construction delays and scarce progress: the finalization after more than ten years of the BTK railway and the conclusion of the first stage of the Alyat port on the Caspian Sea, including the establishment of a free economic zone integrated into the port of Alyat, represent a decisive milestone toward a more integrated regional network and value-added industrial services (Ziyadov, 2012). These projects surely enhance opportunities to tap the potential of the Middle Corridor for rail cargo traffic from China to Europe via the Caspian Sea and Black Sea under the TRACECA corridor. Furthermore, the Azerbaijan Caspian Shipping Company CJSC and Kazakhstan Railways JSC have established a joint venture for cargo transportation along the Middle Corridor. Azerbaijan, Georgia, Kazakhstan, and Ukraine recently announced the creation of a joint venture to introduce the principle of a 'single window' in the processing of goods carried through the Middle Corridor. In June 2017, the Trans-Caspian International Transport Route International Association signed a memorandum of cooperation with the Association of Transport and Communications of China during a meeting of corridor participants in Astana (Tsurkov, 2018). In 2018, new competitive tariffs were announced for transportation along the corridor. Thanks to these efforts, 3.5 million tons and about 15,000 containers are planned to be transported along the corridor from Turkey to Kazakhstan, Central Asia, and China by the end of 2019. According to plans, the Middle Corridor should reach seven to eight million tons of cargo in transportation by 2020 (16 by 2034) and expand the range of transported goods. There are also plans to transport 520,000 tons of oil products, 350,000 tons of grain, 364,000 tons of non-ferrous metals, and 360,000 tons of coal from Kazakhstan along the route in 2018 (Tsurkov, 2018).

The opening of the BTK, the new Alyat port, and better logistics and tariffs can indeed alter the Middle Corridor's situation and position in the competition for additional transcontinental transit container traffic. Indeed, as a result of these efforts, the first Chinese freight train travelled from Xi'an to Europe in November 2019, crossing under Istanbul's Bosporus Strait and marking the beginning of commercial operations along the route (Hürriyet Daily News, 2019).

However, challenges and constraints remain, specifically related to infrastructure issues and poor logistical performance along the route and limited once more by China's ambiguous corridor politics. Regarding technical–infrastructural constraints, while the finalization of BTK represents a major step forward, containers still need to be unloaded many times at the Aktau/Alyat ports and eventually at the Georgian and Rumanian ports. Alternatively, the gauge needs to be changed twice across the overland route (Chinese/Kazakh and Turkish/Georgian border). Moreover, as we will discuss, the lack of a freight-dedicated connection between Kars, Sivas, and Ankara along with missing links in Turkey's east–west rail network represent limitations for the Southern Route and for the Middle Corridor. To this adds a lack of freight wagons, locomotives, and rolling stock as well as a poorly developed Caspian vessels fleet.

In terms of logistics services, with the exception of Turkey, Azerbaijan and Georgia each demonstrate a poor record in logistics, scoring particularly low in custom clearance procedures and infrastructure (The World Bank, 2018b). This fact is reinforced by insufficiently implemented agreements on coordinated tariffs and custom procedures. As a result, the combined effect of poor infrastructure and logistics performance among the involved countries and technical barriers (i.e., unloading and gauge changes) have continued to lead to significantly higher costs per container ($6,000–$7,000; see Table 3.1), which are still non-competitive without Chinese subsidization.

But here, China's role again proves ambiguous: as the main source of transcontinental traffic, China is clearly in search of alternative routes and keen to develop the West China–West Asia corridor, as evidenced by the recent initiation of commercial operations along the corridor (Hürriyet Daily News, 2019). However, Beijing has tended to avoid open support for the Middle Route in an effort to appease Moscow. Because the corridor bypasses the Northern Route entirely, Beijing seems more inclined to step in once the involved countries have shown themselves to be capable of increasing the route's competitiveness rather than simply actively supporting its development. As a result, however, Beijing's approach of silently supporting this route and fostering competition with the Northern Corridor might come at the detriment of greater coordination among continental Eurasian countries.

3.4 The Southern Corridor: the Iran–Turkey route

This is even more true if the Southern Corridor, or the 'Southern Silk Road', is included in the picture. The corridor represents the third option for transcontinental traffic out of China and a potential further competitor to the Northern and Middle Corridors. According to calculations, excluding the already well-developed but increasingly overloaded Northern Route, both the Southern Route ('Southern Silk Road') and the Middle Corridor could attract up to 8% of all Eurasian rail freight until 2027 (Berger, 2017). In terms of volume, roughly 80,000–100,000 TEU could be added and further volumes rerouted from the Northern Route to these two corridors.

Specifically, the Southern Corridor has some key advantages compared to the Northern and Middle Corridors and is being actively developed by China. According to Chinese plans, the Southern Route or 'Southern Silk Road' (Route 4 on the map) starts from central and western China (particularly Chengdu, Chongqing, Yiwu, Urumqi, and Kashgar), crosses Kazakhstan and Turkmenistan along the eastern coast of the Caspian Sea (or, alternatively, is routed via Kazakhstan, Uzbekistan, and Turkmenistan), reaches Iran, and eventually connects to Turkey and Europe.

In 2016, the first container test train from Yiwu to Teheran reached the Iranian capital in only 14 days. New connections were added in the subsequent two years, the latest being a direct and regular train service between Inner Mongolia and Teheran (Noack, 2018) and between Urumqi and Teheran (Sohrabi, 2018). Iran, the key country along the corridor, has particularly ambitious plans for its rail network: with currently 7,500 km of railroad under construction, the declared goal is to extend the national railroad network from less than 15,000 km today to approximately 25,000 km by 2025. According to officials of the Republic of Iran Railways, the expansion will produce almost 12,000 km of new railroad and considerable progress in the fields of electrification and double-tracked lines (Rogers, 2015).

For its part, China's aim is to tap the potential of the Iranian market and profit from east–west transit opportunities to link to Turkey and Europe. As for the Middle and Northern Corridors, this interest has been accompanied by visible investments in Iran's rail infrastructure. In July 2017, for example, China EximBank entered into a $1.5b loan agreement to finance the electrification of the 926 km Tehran–Mashhad main line, a project that will help increase the route's maximum speed to up to 120 km/h for freight trains (250 km/h for passenger trains) and its yearly freight capacity to 10 million tonnes (Railway Gazette International, 2017). In the same year, Chinese companies, led by the China Railway Group Limited, announced the construction of the 375 km long Tehran–Qom–Isfahan high-speed railroad (Financial Tribune, 2017).

The advantages of this route are technical and geo-economic: technically, trains along this route only need to change gauge twice. In fact, except from the Central Asian section of the route, all other involved countries (China, Iran, and Turkey) possess the European standard gauge (1,435 mm).

Geo-economically, with the Northern Route reaching its maximum capacity and the Middle Corridor plagued by technical problems and latent political conflicts, the route could be a valid alternative.

However, existing infrastructural gaps and the political–economic situation in Iran still limit the chance to fully realize the route's potential. For now, while transport along this route is competitive between China and Iran, services must be improved between Iran, Turkey, and Europe. The reason is related to bottlenecks and infrastructure gaps between Iran and Turkey and inside the two countries. At present, rail connections between Western Europe and Iran would still take ten days (Banning and Mani, 2018), with the major bottleneck represented by the missing rail bridge across Lake Van at the Turkish–Iranian border. Ferry services were introduced. From the west end of the lake, a rail ferry carries the train to Van at the eastern end. Newly built ferries can transport a 500 m train (four tracks, 130 m long each) in a single ride at one hour faster than the current ones. However, this bottleneck still decreases speed and timeliness.

Moreover, as reported, railway infrastructure modernization in Iran and Turkey would be required at a much higher speed to align east–west connections in both countries. In Turkey, congestion around Istanbul and the Marmaray Tunnel, the fact that two main east–west transit routes in Turkey are mountainous and equipped with ramps (not electrified) and mostly single-tracked, and the still-missing connection between Sivas and Kars along the Ankara–Kars route all negatively affect the corridor's functionality. In Iran, the situation is even more complicated: the rail network and rolling stock are in desperate need of modernization, electrification, and expansion, yet the government's plans and Chinese investments alone will not compensate for the country's political and economic isolation after sanctions were reimposed. In 2018, Western companies, including rail industry companies like Stadler and Siemens, began cancelling their deals (Handelszeitung, 2018).

Finally, political instability in the Middle East, close to the Iran–Iraq–Turkey border, adds more security risks to the needed infrastructural development. All in all, in the short to medium term, the difficulties of Iran and Turkey to align their respective rail network developments and Iran's isolation could offer a chance for the Middle Corridor to emerge as a bypass for east–west continental transit.

However, the corridor that is openly supported by China (as opposed to the Middle Corridor) crosses two densely populated countries with relatively diversified economies and is strategically located to serve as a rapid gateway to the Middle East, East Africa, and Southeastern Europe and as a bypass from the Indian subcontinent and Southern China. Should Iran's political–diplomatic isolation be overcome and investments flow more rapidly into the rail network of Iran and Turkey, the Southern Corridor could indeed quickly compete with the Northern and Middle Corridors, ultimately emerging as an external competitor to most continental Eurasian countries involved in east–west connections in the long run.

Notes

1 In the absence of official statistics, this is an estimated value based on press reports for the year 2016 as reported by Jakobowski, Poplawski, and Kaczmarski ($22b) and on the author's own calculations based on the further increase in rail traffic for the year 2017. See pp. 27–28 in Jakobowski, J., Poplawski, K., & Kaczmarski, M. (2018). 'The EU-China rail connections: Background, actors, interests' *Center for Eastern Studies*. Available at: www.osw.waw.pl/sites/default/files/studies_72_silk-railroad_net.pdf (Accessed: 10 July 2020).
2 According to the aggregated ranking of the Logistic Performance Index for the years 2012–2018, Kazakhstan, the better-performing country among continental Eurasian countries, ranked only 77th worldwide before Russia (85), Azerbaijan (123), Georgia (124), and Uzbekistan (112).

4 Deepening trade ties with Asia

The future of Eurasia transport integration?

The aforementioned shift in the geographic location of economic activities inside Europe and China, as well as the catalytic role played by the BRI since 2013, have undoubtedly contributed to the establishment of overland transcontinental connections and to the creation of a source of income for continental Eurasian countries. However, transcontinental transit seemingly presents two main limitations to sustainable integration of continental Eurasia in global value chains.

First, as discussed earlier, it potentially fosters competition among routes and countries both within continental Eurasia and with the 'external' route crossing Iran and Turkey, without necessarily supporting much-needed connectivity at the domestic and cross-regional level. In fact, China's strategic decision to consolidate traffic on a few hubs in central China and along fewer corridors while diversifying its logistical access to Europe could potentially jeopardize today's situation, wherein different routes serve different Chinese regions while only the Northern Route serves as a single gateway for Central Europe. While competition might increase efficiency along the corridors, a lack of coordination and cooperation among the three main routes could compromise the development of cross-border regional supply chains – even more so if considering that the three main east–west transport corridors cross EAEU and non-EAEU members, with greater normative and service harmonization the only way to avoid disruptive competition over tariffs and services.

Second, and related to the first point, transit royalties create certain new sources of income for state companies and for the elites without significant positive spillover effects on local employment or the development of local and regional value chains. As recently argued by Lall and Lebrand (2019, p. 2), in Central Asia, transport investments under the BRI, which largely focus on transcontinental arteries of traffic, tend "to bring more spatial concentration, not the dispersion of economic activity within a country"; that is, they lead to agglomeration and clusterization. However, without domestic reforms that foster the mobility of labour, goods, and services and the

Deepening trade ties with Asia 35

expansion of a domestic transport network, spatial economic imbalances within countries in continental Eurasia will increase.

Given this backdrop, Europe has long warned against this development and, with its recent connectivity strategy (European Union External Action Service, 2018), has attempted to offer a more sustainable model of transcontinental connectivity conducive to participation in domestic and regional value chains. However, a mix of geographic proximity and financial firepower has given China a competitive advantage in continental Eurasia. As a result, China seemingly offers more chances for continental Eurasia to participate in advanced regional value chains. This fact is clearly reinforced by underdeveloped relations between the EU and EAEU.

4.1 The rise of Eurasian-Asian trade

When it comes to redrawing the economic geography and infrastructure orientation of continental Eurasia, China's emerging role as an alternative to Europe becomes evident when comparing the relevance the country has assumed for continental Eurasia in terms of trade. Without a doubt, continental Eurasia's main trade partner remains Europe; however, since the early 2000s, ties between single sub-regions of the greater Eurasian space (specifically among developing Asia; the Middle East, including Iran and Turkey; Eastern Europe and Central Asia; and Russia on one side and China on the other) have expanded dramatically at different levels and speeds (Figure 4.1). As of 2017, China's exports to this vast space, which includes

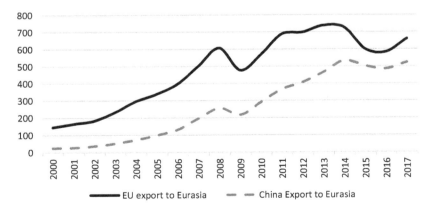

Figure 4.1 EU and China exports to broader Eurasia (including CIS, developing Asia, the Middle East, Iran, and Turkey), in billion US dollars, 2000–2017

Data source: International Monetary Fund, Direction of Trade Statistics; author's own graph

36 Deepening trade ties with Asia

but is not limited to continental Eurasia and stretches from Southeast Asia to west Asia and Eastern Europe, have almost equalled exports from the EU. At the same time, exports (mainly energy or energy products) from Greater Eurasia to China have been rapidly catching up with exports to the EU (Figure 4.2). A Eurasian–Asian sub-regional system of trade relations has thus emerged, largely decoupling from the West and Europe.

In a long-term perspective, this trend indicates an acceleration in value chains regionalization paths and desynchronization between OECD and non-OECD developing economies, which largely predates recent events like the COVID pandemic or more recent protectionist tends. In fact, according to the OECD, particularly Asia and Africa, thanks to rapid economic growth, will substantially increase their share of global trade after 2030. Consequently, trade within the euro area will slow down, trade within the OECD area will halve, and trade among non-OECD economies will more than double. Emerging economies will increase their manufacturing share and move up the value chains, with a direct impact on private consumption and investments and a greater concentration of production and consumption away from developed and toward developing economies.

The major impact of this radical shift in growth, production, and trade path will be on freight volumes and routes across Eurasia. By 2050, as the localization of production and consumption will shift eastwards and southwards, the Asia–Africa trade nexus along the greater Indian Ocean and intra-Asian

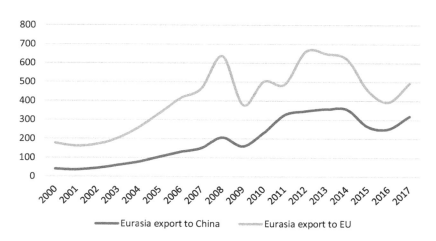

Figure 4.2 Broader Eurasia (including CIS, developing Asia, the Middle East, Iran, and Turkey) exports to EU and China, in billion US dollars, 2000–2017

Source: International Monetary Fund, Direction of Trade Statistics; author's own graph

overland connections are expected to grow over-proportionally, and with them international freight volume is expected to be significantly stronger along maritime routes of the Indian Ocean and inland connections in Asia. Growth in freight volumes on the transpacific and the transatlantic routes will slow down, while major increases in freight volumes from China to Europe are expected to occur. This will have a major impact on the Indian Ocean (+700%) and Mediterranean/Caspian freight routes (+280%). However, an equally significant increase in freight volumes is expected in intraregional freight flows by road and rail within the Asian (+403%) and African continent (+400%) and – even more significant – between Asia and Africa (+406%) (International Transport Forum, 2019, pp. 34–38).

Against this backdrop, continental Eurasia finds itself in a potentially privileged position as it can profit from growing trade ties with Asia and from participation in its value chains with China's BRI initiative acting as a catalyst to connect Afro-Eurasian production networks.

To be sure, compared with other regions of broader Eurasia, the share of countries in continental Eurasia (including Russia) relative to China's exports and imports is still much lower than, for example, the share of developing Asia and the Middle East. As discussed, continental Eurasia remains relatively isolated from Asia's value chains, as opposed to Southeast Asia – yet it is too distant from open oceans, sea trade lines, and ports to easily expand its trade with Asia, as in the case of the Middle East.

However, the reorientation of China's trade toward the entire, broader Eurasian continent, including its continental portion, shows that Beijing's major interest consists of diversifying its energy supplies and the final markets for its goods by expanding its production networks. This clearly happens by expanding its presence in what Beijing sees as a single, interconnected developing market and eventual production platform stretching from Asia across Eurasia to Africa. Today, China's interest in penetrating new markets has been accelerated by the trade conflict with the United States and by increasingly difficult relations with the EU. In light of these circumstances, new inland manufacturing centres and shorter overland distances across the continent allow Beijing greater flexibility, ultimately accelerating the multimodal integration of continental Eurasia in what is supposed to become a China-dominated transregional production network.

4.2 The rise of Asia's FDI in continental Eurasia: first steps, future trend?

A major impact on the creation of cross-regional value chains in continental Eurasia comes from China's rising FDI. As reported by the latest Eurasian Development Bank report (2017) on direct investments in continental

Eurasia, Asian countries are indeed expanding their presence in continental Eurasia, despite starting from a much lower level than Europe's FDI.

To be sure, the EU is a major source of investment in continental Eurasia in general and in the EAEU specifically, targeting Russia in particular. Between 2010 and 2017, European countries provided the bulk of foreign investments in Russia, accounting for 87% of GDP in the EAEU and serving as the major economy in continental Eurasia (Kofner, 2019). In 2017, EU's FDI in Russia amounted to more than €200b (European Commission, 2020b).

Moreover, the economic structure of the EU and of many continental Eurasian countries, particularly members of the EAEU, is highly compatible, as the latter export raw materials and minerals and import mainly final consumer goods or capital goods. However, the combined effect of Russian–European sanctions following the Ukraine crisis and the lack of political–commercial and trade cooperation between the EU and the EAEU is seriously limiting the potential to further integrate the supply and value chains of continental Eurasia into the production network of the Central European manufacturing core, thus fully taking advantage of the eastward shift in economic activities and of improved logistics and transport services.

Conversely, rising trade ties between China on one side and continental Eurasia on the other are increasingly facilitated by an institutional–legal framework. China and the EAEU recently signed a non-preferential trade agreement, which, while still needing to define product categories and not necessarily implying an automatic reduction of tariff barriers or creation of a free trade area, represents a first legal step toward trade facilitation that is lacking in the case of relations with the EU (Shilina, 2019).

Meanwhile, as China attempts to diversify its value chains and its final markets across broader Eurasia, the structure of its exports and the quantity and quality of its FDI are changing as well. For example, capital and manufacturing goods have come to play increasingly important roles in the structure of Chinese exports to continental Eurasia, with a particular increase since the outbreak of the economic and financial crisis in 2008 (Pepe, 2018). According to the Eurasian Development Bank (2017), China remains the primary source of investment from Asia to the EAEU and other states within the Commonwealth of Independent States (CIS), constantly expanding its presence. FDI stock accumulated by Chinese transnational corporations in the five EAEU countries, Azerbaijan, Tajikistan, and Ukraine amounted to $33.7b (Eurasian Development Bank, 2017) compared to less than $11b in 2008 (Vinokurov, 2018).

The Eurasian Development Bank (2017) further reported that China has traditionally targeted the oil and gas industry, with a share close to 74% of the total stock of outward investment in eight selected post-Soviet countries for the year 2016. However, this share has followed a persistent downward trend, while a significant inflow of investment capital into construction and mechanical engineering, agriculture and food products (i.e., processing of agricultural raw materials), and rail and road connectivity has slowly but persistently occurred over the last six years (Eurasian Development Bank, 2017).

By 2019, for instance, the cumulative number of China projects since the launch of the BRI in Central Asia's manufacturing and agricultural industry (66) was already higher than in the oil and gas industry (44), totalling $15m. The number of projects in rail and road connectivity (51) exceeded those related to energy connectivity (47). In terms of value, while investments in energy connectivity and in the oil and gas industry reached nearly $90m, the cumulative stock of investments in the rail and road sector, non-energy manufacturing, and agriculture and food processing industry reached almost $55m compared to being nearly non-existent before the launch of the BRI (Vakulchuk et al., 2019, pp. 3–4).

China has also geographically diversified its activities beyond Central Asia, reducing its focus on Kazakhstan and directing increasing investments toward Russia, Belarus, and Ukraine (Eurasian Development Bank, 2017). In the case of Belarus, for example, overall Chinese investments in transport and mechanical engineering accounted for 34% and 27%, respectively, of all Chinese outward FDI stock in Belarus (Eurasian Development Bank, 2017), mostly directed toward the 'Great Stone' logistic-industrial park strategically located along the northern transport corridor to Europe. Here, a small but significant example of emerging Eurasian–Chinese value chains is the Chinese–Belarus JV BelGee, which produces semi-knocked-down assembly of Geely motor vehicles and has been accorded the status of a local manufacturer able to engage in duty-free exports of parts and components from Belarus to other EAEU countries, primarily Russia (Belarus News, 2019b).

While this is a far-to-come scenario and problems with the development of the Russian Far East and Central Asia transport infrastructure to the east are paramount (see later), an increase and diversification of China's FDI into continental Eurasia's manufacturing and non-energy sectors is already visible, with potential effects on the establishment of cross-regional value chains.

All in all, geographic proximity, increasing Chinese activities in continental Eurasia, a geographic reorientation of trade and investment flows matched by the absence of a legal framework for investments and technology transfer between the EU and the EAEU, and the first trade agreement – though 'non-preferential' – signed by the EAEU and China in 2019, all represent steps toward a general reorientation of the economic geography of continental Eurasia toward the Asia Pacific. For instance, it has been calculated that the implementation of the current non-preferential trade agreement, that is, the elimination of non-trade barriers with China, would over-proportionally advantage the Eurasian Economic Union with a net welfare effect of USD 5.7 billion (0.3% of GPD), and the gross welfare effect of USD 8.9 billion (Kofner, 2020b)

4.3 Current limits and risks of Eurasia's transport integration in Asia's value and supply chains

Even with these promising developments and plans, a mismatch between potential and reality persist in the short to medium term, particularly when it comes to cross-border transport integration. First, while FDI from China in continental Eurasia's manufacturing sector is on the rise and has the potential to eventually become a 'game changer', for the time being, the level still remains too low to represent a serious instrument to durably and homogeneously integrate continental Eurasia into value-added production networks – even more so when considering that FDI from other Asian countries like Singapore, Japan, and South Korea remains either negligible or primarily directed toward the oil and gas sector, as in the case of Japan. In general, investments from Asia in the EAEU and other CIS countries are only a portion of Europe's FDI.

Moreover, even a deeper and comprehensive free trade agreement between Beijing and the Eurasian Economic Union, which would provide for a reduction in both tariffs and non-tariff barriers and potentially favour FDI flows from China, would only reinforce the asymmetry in the trade structure between the Union and China. As Yuri Kofner calculates (Kofner, 2020b), while such an agreement would have the highest effect on EAEU's welfare and significantly increase exports to China (by about USD 35 billion), China's exports to the EAEU would increase most in total value terms in high-value-added sectors like – among others – electric machinery, chemicals, non-electric machinery, manufactured articles, and transport equipment. Conversely, the increase in EAEU exports to China would largely happen in the primary sector of the industry and in low-value-added manufacturing (with the exception of chemical products) – petroleum, metals, minerals and precious stones, wood, and non-electric machinery. Therefore, a liberalization of bilateral trade would scarcely contribute to a diversification of the economies of the EAEU countries.

Second, the agglomeration effects that have followed the inland shift in value chains, production, and transport networks inside China have clearly been favoured by large and cheap labour present in the central regions and by a high degree of demographic-urban concentration in central China.

These factors have created macro-regional areas of industrial and urban development like Chongqing or Chengdu. The same effect might be difficult to replicate in western China and continental Eurasia, whose population is scattered across vast, largely rural areas and enormous distances. As in the case of transcontinental corridors, without proper reforms to favour the movement of labour and goods and services, improved cross-border transportation links between China and continental Eurasia might well prove instrumental to 'clusterization' and industrial activity concentration, which could end up attracting further Asian and Chinese investments. This is in fact the main idea behind the establishment of special economic zones, as in the case of advanced special economic zones in the Russian Far East or in countries like Belarus, Uzbekistan, Kazakhstan, and Azerbaijan.

However, without domestic structural reform and improvements to intranational transportation links between cities and rural areas, this development might merely exacerbate regional inequalities by concentrating economic activity and labour in bigger cities near border-crossing points or along transregional corridors (Lall and Lebrand, 2019). While industrialization will foster urbanization, it might also lead to the abandonment of rural areas, posing economic, social, and security risks to many central Eurasian countries.

Third, low land prices and high public investments in transport infrastructure have guaranteed a high level of growth in new central Chinese provinces for the past 15–20 years and proved pivotal to the establishment of transcontinental rail services across continental Eurasia. However, increasing land prices and labour costs in these new manufacturing hubs could lead to further relocation of activities in the long term, either further west, toward continental Eurasia (with indeed positive effects on this space), or, more probably, further south toward southeastern Asia, where demographic and industrial activities are already concentrated and producers are closer to future final consumers. The latter scenario might become more realistic after the signature of the Regional Comprehensive Economic Partnership in November 2020 (see more in Chapter 5). In this case, continental Eurasia would need to compete with Southeast Asia over Chinese FDI and risk being only marginally integrated into Asia's production networks.

Fourth, and directly related to the question of transport integration, while "the BRI transport corridors can 'sew' the Eurasian macro-region together" (Vinokurov, 2018, p. 134), they can also increase competition among Eurasian countries, both over the role as transit gateways and over additional FDI from Asia. This is particularly apparent in the case of Kazakhstan and Russia: considering the flow of goods between Russia and China, only 2% transits through Central Asia, whereas 86% of goods traded between Kazakhstan and China are supplied by land transport crossing the border between the two countries; the remaining 14% comes via Russian ports (Vinokurov, 2018). With China relocating production activities and consolidation hubs toward central China, a modernization and improvement of services along the New Eurasian Land Bridge will lead to a traffic diversion, potentially increasing the share of Russian–Chinese trade crossing Central Asia but bypassing the Russian Far East ports and Eastern and Central Siberia (Vinokurov, 2018).

Specifically, the newly established corridor through Kazakhstan and China can attract new traffic from the manufacturing centre of central and southwestern China and, potentially, traffic from eastern China and East Asia via the corridor extension to the Chinese port of Lianyungang (i.e., New Eurasian Land Bridge). Conversely, the Trans-Siberian line is far too north to be able to attract new traffic other than from northeastern and northern China. While the Trans-Siberian–Trans-Mongolian route will not lose traffic from northeastern China, it will not be able to attract additional traffic from other Chinese regions. This would prove particularly detrimental for Russia's Far East development plans: Russia's 'Pivot to Asia' is inherently linked with the Far East Development Program, both of which depend heavily on successful implementation of the upgrade and expansion of the central Siberian and Far East transport infrastructure to attract additional FDI in these regions. By doing so, Russia's government hopes to achieve three main goals: increase transit along the Northern Corridor from the Far East ports to Europe, crossing the far east and central Siberian territories; and leverage the upgraded performance of the Trans-Siberian line to accelerate integration of Siberia and the Far East into Asia-Pacific value chains by attracting Asian investments while, in the meantime, increasing raw materials exports to Asia (Pepe, 2019).

Formal cooperation notwithstanding, neither the EAEU nor the BRI has thus far proven able to enhance regional development in the Far East of Russia and in the northeast of China. While China and Russia have agreed on the establishment of a joint fund for the development of China's northeastern provinces and the Russian Far East in 2017 (Xinhua, 2017), the BRI corridors, as discussed, completely bypass the Far Eastern ports and the eastern section of the (Transsiberian Railline), indicating the marginal relevance China attaches to continental northeast Asia within the BRI framework.

Overall, as previously shown in this study, while the Trans-Siberian line can hardly be entirely bypassed, its role as an exclusive Eurasian 'land bridge' is indeed eroding along with the chance to divert new generated westbound traffic through the Russian Far East. As a result, Moscow depends on functional transport integration with the rail and logistics network of Central Asian countries, specifically with Kazakhstan.

However, the Kazak transport system retains its formal independence; the country's strategy for the diversification of its transport routes ('New Silk Way') and industrial basis (Nurly Zhol) is only partially aligned to Moscow's strategic interests, as evidenced by the opening of the New Eurasian Land Bridge from the Chinese port of Lianyungang as well as the Middle Corridor. For its part, Kazakhstan might be negatively affected by the Southern Corridor, which could end up crossing southern Central Asia and Uzbekistan, thus bypassing the Kazakh territory. Under these circumstances, competition over routes between continental Eurasian countries, and specifically between two key members of the EAEU, could exacerbate competition over market access and FDI from China and Asia.

5 COVID-19 and the evolving EU–China relation

Game changer for Eurasia transport integration?

5.1 COVID-19: a trend accelerator

The outbreak of the COVID-19 pandemic in early 2020 has deeply affected the globalized world economy by disrupting the complex web of cross-border elongated value and supply chains. The pandemic has also unleashed a political wave calling for more supply chain resilience, production repatriation, and more independence from China's supplies.

While it is too soon to predict the long-term impact of COVID-19 on Eurasia transport integration, the pandemic is predicted to alter – at least partially – the picture sketched in the previous chapters. From the perspective of continental Eurasia's integration in global and continental value and supply chains, the COVID-19 pandemic's long-term implications are mixed, bearing both chances and risks. In fact, COVID-19 has impacted primarily the relation between the two major manufacturing powerhouses, the EU and China, changing the reciprocal perception about the economic interdependence created in the past two decades across Eurasia. While it has deepened trends toward regionalization, it has to date, however, not fundamentally reduced this interdependence.

At first glance, the immediate effect of COVID-19 on Eurasia overland transport corridors has been even positive. Between January and March 2020, in the weeks and months immediately after the pandemic outbreak in China and its rapid spread in other Asian countries, borders across Eurasia were shut down, factories closed, and supply chains thrown into disarray, with massive limitations to transcontinental transport services, particularly truck transportation.

However, the surge in air shipping prices and transit times in air and ocean freight has increased the competitiveness of transcontinental rail services between Asia and Europe. According to DB Cargo Eurasia, already by the end of March, no transcontinental service was interrupted between China and Europe, and border-crossing points remained in regular operation mode

(DB Cargo, 2020). By June 2020, according to the United Transport and Logistics Company–Eurasian Rail Alliance (UTLC ERA), the shipment of loaded containers to China doubled compared to the same month of 2019, with a total of 34,000 TEUs of loaded containers shipped to Europe (van Leijen, 2020a).

Moreover, the COVID-19 pandemic has seemingly positively affected volumes of traffic along the Middle Corridor, particularly for transregional connections. Following the pandemic outbreak, many neighbouring countries have closed their border to Iran, which is the main transit route for cargo between Central Asia and Turkey. With the Iranian borders closed, traffic from China and Central Asia to Turkey has been redirected from the Turkmen–Iranian–Turkish route to the trans-Caspian corridor, with new services entering into operation during the peak months of the pandemic (Veliyev, 2020; van Leijen, 2020b). This unexpected boost could indeed partially change the volume balance among three east–west corridors described in chapter three in favour of the middle route.

While in the short term COVID-19 might have positively affected long-distance rail services across Eurasia, it has however also doubtless induced a new dynamic in the relation between Eurasia's two major manufacturing powerhouses and drivers of Eurasia transport and industrial integration, the EU and China. The dynamic evolution of this relation is set to have a much bigger and durable impact on continental Eurasia than the short-term gains deriving from the increase in transcontinental rail services induced by the pandemic.

To be sure, COVID-19 has not fundamentally altered the logic of Eurasia transport integration as described in the previous chapters. It, however, has inserted new dynamism in the relation between the EU, China, and continental Eurasia as it has accelerated three major trends already unfolding long before the pandemic. These trends have emerged in parallel to the globalization and 'continentalization' of production described in Chapter 2 and are deemed to impact both the direction of trade flows and the location of production network. These are, first, the re-regionalization and consolidation of global value chains (Economist Intelligence Unit, 2020); second, the geo-politicization of trade and industrial policies; third, the long-term emergence of Southeast Asia (and India) as the next poles of growth, production, and consumption next to China. This is part of the more general shift from a transatlantic to an Asian-centred world economic system.

Trends toward a regionalization of production and a geo-politicization of trade and industrial policies dates back to the years before the pandemic. These are the result of both political choices (protectionist and mercantilist approaches mainly following the election of the Trump administration in the US and the more clear emergence of the US–China techno-political rivalry) and technological–economic factors (the digitalization of production, the shortening of supply chains, and the emergence of Asia as the major source of growth, production, and consumption). As reported with succinct clarity by a 2019 OECD report:

> In recent years trade restrictions have increased, and there is now a tendency to prefer bilateral agreements over multilateral trade accords. The global outsourcing model is showing signs of its limitations and manufacturing has become more regionalised... [Developing] Economies are also moving up in the value chain, resulting in an increase in the domestic value-added component of exports. Physical limitations on the fragmentation of global value chains also exist, and there is evidence that global supply chains are consolidating.
>
> (International Transport Forum, 2019, p. 34)

Doubtless, as data and figures presented in Chapter 4 show, the creation of a Eurasian-Asian macro-regional economic and production space centred on China's value chains which largely bypasses the West and Europe is the result of trade flows shifts occurring in the past 15 years but more decisively since the 2008 financial and economic crisis. However, the centrality of China in Asian production networks and growth is not a phenomenon set to endure in the long term. In fact, in 2019 the OECD projected a long-term shift in demography, growth, and production paths not only from West to East – from OECD-developed economies to non-OECD developing countries – but also, inside emerging Asia, from China to India and the rest of Southeast Asia. The latter will gradually take over from China as the engines of global growth (OECD, 2019, p. 62). For instance, the OECD share in global GDP is projected to fall to 31% in 2060, from 44% in 2017 and 61% in 2000. Meanwhile, in the same period the share of non-OECD Southeast Asia is projected to increase from 35% to 46% (OECD, 2019, p. 35).

All in all, by disrupting elongated global value chains, COVID 19 has not only reinforced ongoing trends but – by doing so – it has also exacerbated the geo-economic competition between Europe and China, as calls for a repatriation of economic activities, greater industrial sovereignty, and a diversification of trade ties have become louder.

5.2 The EU between overreliance on China and strategic autonomy: back to Europe?

In Europe, the pandemic has augmented the geopolitical–conflictual nature of the European–Chinese relation by exposing the vulnerability of the EU's elongated value chains as well as the risks of overreliance on China. During the early months of the pandemic, the European Union has therefore sketched out a more self-confident and active policy strategy toward China. While the debate both inside national governments and in the European Commission about the necessity to reaffirm European industrial sovereignty did not start with the COVID-19 outbreak, the pandemic has acted as a catalyst and an accelerator.

For the past few years, public and confidential discussions at both national and European levels have been ongoing, culminating in the French-German Industrial Policy Manifesto of early 2019. In the manifesto, both countries pledged for a strong European industrial policy to foster innovation in new key sectors like health, energy, climate, security, and digital technology (AI) (German Federal Ministry for Economy and Energy; French Ministry of Economy and Finances, 2019).

The move was largely triggered by the security and economic risks related to China's attempts to dominate high-value-added manufacturing (e.g., e-vehicles, including battery production, renewable energies value chains, artificial intelligence and robots, and high-speed trains) and new digital technologies (5G) and acquire strategic assets in Europe, particularly 5G digital networks, power grids, rail, ports, and logistics providers.

However, it was not until COVID-19 that the European debate moved from reflecting on the competitiveness of its own economic–industrial model and the need to nurture production at home to increasingly considering the vulnerability related to the over-reliance on globalized production networks and on China.

The evolving European stance has been determined by the combined effect of the persisting China threat, by the intensifying US–Chinese trade war (and the Trump administration's decoupling attempts), and by the crisis of the liberal globalization and trade governance institutions.

Doubtless, the Trump administration's policy goal to re-shore production has been a major reason for Europe's discomfort, as it aimed not only against Chinese producers but also against European manufacturers. The Trump administration proved willing to use trade-distorting instruments like duties and to put pressure on European governments to align with Washington's new assertive industrial, energy, and digital strategy vis-à-vis both China and Russia. This has contributed to an increased perception among Europeans that their production model based on globally elongated, complex supply chains is particularly vulnerable to geopolitical shocks and needs to be rethought, also vis-à-vis a dramatic redefinition and reassessment of the transatlantic partnership.

Against the backdrop of a changing transatlantic relation and in absence of a coordinated approach toward Beijing, China is increasingly becoming a major concern to the EU. The country emerged not only as a major supplier of intermediate goods for European industry (particularly medical-pharmaceutical, electronic, and automotive) but also as an increasingly competitive provider of new technologies and high-value-added manufacturing. Beijing is also becoming a standard setter in sectors in which European business has lost competitive advantages and in some cases the technological edge (5G technologies).

In this sense, the COVID-19 pandemic has clearly acted as an accelerator, showing the pressing need to produce critical goods in Europe; to invest in strategic value chains, particularly for pharmaceuticals, e-vehicles, and low-carbon or no-carbon energy technologies; and to reduce over-dependency on China.

During the early months of the pandemic, the EU has instituted a more strategic and coordinated approach to industrial policy (European Commission, 2020c, 2020d) to ensure what has been defined as the EU's 'strategic autonomy', that is, greater resilience of the supply and value chains of European companies and infrastructure.

The instruments identified a mix of public investments in low-carbon and no-carbon technologies in line with the Green Deal to repatriate the production of some critical goods, the full realization of the potential of robotization and digitalization of production, which enables re-localization of activities, and an effective screening of China's foreign direct investments at the European level.

To implement these grand schemes, the EU budget deal for the period 2021–2027 reached by the European Council in July 2020 and agreed upon by the EU Parliament and member states in November 2020 includes a one-time €750 billion post-pandemic recovery fund named 'Next Generation EU' (NGEU) (European Commission, 2020e). For instance, as part of the new budget, the Recovery and Resilience Facility, rescEU, and a new health programme, EU4Health, will financially support greater resilience of Europe's industry in the post-pandemic recovery years and – among others – enhance independence from China's supplies.

5.3 China's adjustment to a changing reality: the BRI between 'dual circulation' and Asia's free trade agreement

Amid the pandemic, China has grown increasingly aware of the accelerated transformation brought about by COVID-19 and has reacted accordingly to both seize short-term opportunities and prevent long-term risks.

At first glance, the country has overcome the pandemic faster and sooner than have Europe and the US and seems set to turn into the true winner of the pandemic year 2020. By the end of 2020, the economy was growing again, reaching 4.9% from the 2019 level. So was industrial production (6.9%) and investments (0.8%). With the virus almost disappeared and factories quickly reopening, China's export boomed in September and October 2020 to its highest level since 2019. In October 2020 exports rose by 11.4% on a year-to-year basis after it had increased by 9.9% increase in September. The COVID-induced global demand for medical equipment and electronic products in particular has driven the export of medical equipment and electronics products (Hale, 2020). According to the OECD, in 2021 China is expected to grow at 8%, while the US and Europe will experience a slower path to recovery with growth at around 4%–5% (OECD, 2020).

However, Beijing's very success in coping with COVID-19 and the country's quick recovery is also the reason that several partners, particularly in Europe, have grown increasingly suspicious of the country's technological, industrial, and political offensive which has followed the outbreak. First, the disruption in supplies of medical equipment has severely damaged China's image as a reliable supplier of industrial goods, particularly in Europe (Cerulus, 2020). Then, Beijing's aggressive diplomatic efforts to develop a post-COVID narrative conducive to its geopolitical goals has increased the opposition to the country's initiatives. Both elements have induced – de facto – an acceleration in diversification attempts both in Europe and in Asia.

Conversely, China's outbound investment in Europe in the first quarter of 2020, already declining in 2019 following tightening screening mechanisms in Europe and capital outflow limitations at home, has reached its lowest volume in almost a decade (Rhodium Group, 2020).

Against this backdrop, the BRI initiative – the most visible project of China's ambitions – has been hit particularly hard by COVID-19, with major political–economic ramifications. The economic lockdown and the impossibility of physical mobility have put several infrastructure projects on hold. With a shift from physical to digital connections, the impossibility of physical exchange, and an acceleration in the localization of production by both reshoring attempts and production digitalization, BRI investments have suffered dramatically (Buckley, 2020). In the first six months of 2020, for example, overall BRI-related investment dropped by about 50% from USD 46 billion invested during the first six months of 2019 (and dropping by 60% compared to the first six months of 2018), with a particularly strong decline in West and East Asia (American Enterprise Institute, 2020). In the long term, it is highly probable that several BRI-related projects will not be resumed as the Chinese development banks, the Silk Road Fund, the New Development Bank, and to a certain extent the Asian Infrastructure Investment Bank, might decide to stop funding amid adverse conditions and contract terminations in the host countries.

Confronted with mounting opposition in Europe, a difficult economic environment along the BRI, and pressure by the US's aggressive decoupling attempts, during the course of the pandemic China has hence decisively modified and adapted its foreign and domestic economic strategy to become industrially and economically more self-reliant without abandoning its presence in the global markets.

This implies an announced revision of its economic development model and a decisive re-focusing on deepening trade and industrial relations within Asia, the latter via the long-awaited finalization of the free trade agreement with ASEAN, Japan, Korea, Australia, and New Zealand.

The new concept of the 'dual economic circulation', discussed and included in China's 14th five-year plan at the end of October 2020, stresses the primary role that domestic production and consumption should play in the coming years while calling for increasing the promotion of its own technology and industrial standards ('China Standards 2035') (Koty, 2020) and high-value-added products abroad (Daryl and Sicong, 2020). The concept aims at prioritizing domestic production, consumption, and supply chains (internal circulation) in order to be less vulnerable to external shocks and disruption while remaining engaged in the global markets (external circulation), starting with the immediate neighbourhood.

Meanwhile, China has attempted to strengthen its grip on Asia's value and supply chains and markets. In this sense, the major ASEAN-led and China-backed pan-Asian free trade agreement (Regional Economic Comprehensive Economic Partnership Agreement or RCEP) signed in November 2020 after eight years of hard negotiations between the ten nations of ASEAN plus Japan, China, South Korea, Australia, and New Zealand marks a major step toward greater intra-industrial, cross-border value chains integration in the Asia Pacific (ASEAN, 2020a).

The pact – which covers a market of 2.2 billion people with a combined size of US $26.2 trillion or 30% of the world's GDP – lowers tariffs (in some cases up to 90%), opens up the service trade, and sets common trade rules, including rules of origin within the bloc covering trade, services, investment, e-commerce, telecommunications, and copyright (ASEAN, 2020b).

The pact is a key geopolitical and geo-economic achievement for China, as it leaves the US (and Europe) out, keeps Japan and ASEAN in, and does not include India. Doubtless, in the short term – considering the size of the Chinese economy – it might very well increase China's grip on regional value chains and markets and testifies to the growing relevance of macro-regional trade blocs and production regionalization post-COVID. Issues like industrial subsidies and state-owned enterprises are not addressed by the RCEP, and the pact does not include any environmental or social standard chapters. Both elements doubtless allow China's state capitalism model to expand further in Asia. As calculated (Petri and Plummer, 2020), China could gain the most from the pact ($100 billion) by 2030, followed by Japan ($46 billion), South Korea ($23 billion), and Southeast Asia ($19 billion). Contrary to common assumptions, however, we state that the pact also comes at a price for Beijing. By creating common rules of origin for the whole bloc (ASEAN, 2020c Chapter 3), one country-of-origin certificate will suffice for shipping goods across the bloc and reduce transaction costs, allowing companies greater flexibility in designing their supply and value chains. While this rule will doubtless favour China's companies in entering other Asian markets, it also helps companies of other Asian advanced economies like Japan and Korea to create their own value and supply chains independent from China, particularly in the ASEAN markets, while increasing competition for Chinese companies both on the Chinese and on third markets (Garcia-Herrero, 2020). Moreover, thanks to a clause allowing Delhi to re-enter the deal, the RCEP leaves a window open for India, whose participation would doubtless make the pact much less Sino-centred. Consequently, the pact, while certainly favourable to China – is more a compromise than a sign of China's exclusive dominance and in the long run can be expected to dilute rather than strengthen China's position in Asia's production networks.

In fact, even before the pact China was already facing a dilemma in Asia, accelerated by the effects of COVID-19. On the one side, foreign companies – European, American, and Japanese, for both political (diversification and decoupling) and economic (rising labour costs) reasons – accelerated the relocation of production outside China (Forbes, 2020). On the other side, Chinese companies are called on to re-shore their own supply and value chains inside China, following the new 'dual circulation' principle, while they themselves might need to relocate labour-intensive activities in the direct neighbourhood, particularly in South Asia, as domestic labour costs rise.

Against this backdrop, by lowering tariffs and setting common trade rules, the RCEP will leave Chinese companies exposed to greater competition on the domestic market (for example, the RCEP lowers tariffs on Japan's export – parts and components – to China by 86%) (Gakuto, 2020). It will, however, also accelerate the already ongoing intra-Asia competition over the re-localization of regional supply and value chains in low-cost ASEAN countries. These countries are indeed set to become the next geo-economic battlefield, as shown by Japan's (Reynolds and Urabe, 2020) and Korea's (Suk-yee, 2020) relocation attempts toward Southeast Asia, the more recent EU–Vietnam free trade agreement (European Commission, 2020f), and even the renewed European interest for cooperation with ASEAN (EEAS, 2020).

As a result, while China's centrality as Asia's workbench might be challenged, Beijing will also face competition by Japan (Abe, 2020), Korea, and potentially by India (should Delhi decide to re-enter the deal) on the ASEAN markets.

Against the backdrop of these developments in Asia and the COVID-induced backlash, China will necessarily need to restructure but not give up on the BRI, as its very logic is linked to domestic calculations of political, ethnic, and economic balance. In fact, the BRI plays a crucial role both in the concept of the 'dual economic circulation' – as it will prove functional to strengthen China's dominated but more self-reliant and resilient supply and value chains – and as an instrument to accelerate China's access into third markets beyond Asia, in continental Eurasia, the Middle East, and West Asia.

In the long term, the project is therefore presumably set to be streamlined and re-focused on digital technologies (5G networks) – the 'Digital Silk Road', medical and pharmaceuticals (the 'Health Silk Road'), and green and low-carbon value chains (wind, solar, and hydrogen; 'Greening the BRI') and will also focus – parallel to transport infrastructure –on electric grids and power connectivity (Global Energy Interconnection Initiative).

5.4 Implications for Eurasia's transport integration

Against this backdrop, the COVID-induced changes in the EU's and China's approach to supply and value chains can be expected to impact Eurasia's transport integration, at both transcontinental and transregional levels, in four major ways:

First, at the transcontinental level, notwithstanding the adjustments in the EU–China relation and reciprocal decoupling and reshoring attempts, industrial–technological ties between Eurasia's two major manufacturing powerhouses will remain strong in the short to medium term, and so will transcontinental supply chains and rail services. In fact, both the EU and China still need each other as a source of industrial expertise, technology, intermediate industrial goods, and final markets. This fact and the already existing inland shift in the geographic localization of economic activities in both blocs will not significantly alter the logic of transcontinental transport across continental Eurasia as it has developed in the past decade.

Second, continental Eurasia presumably will become in the short to medium term even more dependent on Asia for investments and as a final market, especially considering the asymmetric recovery paths in Europe and the West and Europe's current inward-looking recovery strategy. Specifically, this might lead to an increase in continental Eurasia's economic and technological dependence on China. China's ambiguous approach to investments and corridors across continental Eurasia will presumably grow while the Chinese–Russia relation is set to deepen but also become increasingly asymmetrical, narrowing Moscow's space of (geopolitical) manoeuvre (Gabuev, 2020).

Chinese companies' repatriation of production activities in the immediate neighbourhood will go along with a mix of consolidation of cross-regional value chains, transport hubs, and terminals and the creation of redundancies to have rapid and quick back-up solutions. Following the RCEP, Beijing might increasingly focus on Southeast Asia. This fact will presumably reinforce the role of Southeast Asia as a privileged destination of Chinese FDI as opposed to continental Eurasia (as discussed in Chapter 4). While domestic Chinese companies, challenged by foreign competitors at home and in the ASEAN countries, could still turn to continental Eurasia for relocating labour-intensive economic activities or expanding their production network from central China further west, continental Eurasia might end up playing a complementary role in China's high-end value and supply chains. Meanwhile, the continent's economic dependence on China will grow. The combined effect of these two phenomena will only increase competition among central Asian countries and Russia over routes, terminals, and industrial value chains.

Third, while this is true, continental Eurasia might benefit from the accelerated competition and diversification inside Asia. As foreign (including Japanese, Korean, and European) companies relocate production outside China, China's stance in Asia's value and supply chains is set to change in the long term. While China will remain essential for continental Eurasia's transport and economic integration, shifting political interests and perceptions in both Europe and Asia and growing competition from other Asian countries will accelerate the geographic diversification and re-localization of supply and value chains, both in Asia and *across* Eurasia. This will make the post-COVID Eurasia transport equation less Sino-centric and BRI-driven and more diversified and competitive.

In fact, in the long term, growth, technological innovation, industrial development, and consumer markets will increasingly gravitate to the Indo-Pacific macro-region and eventually along the Southeast Asia–India–West Asia–Africa nexus, as the RCEP agreement shows. This opens up greater – and unexpected – chances for continental Eurasia and for the Eurasian Economic Union to attract investments in advanced manufacturing sectors and logistics from Asian countries other than China. For more detached regions of continental Eurasia like Central Asia or the Russian Far East and Northeast Asia, this will also imply greater efforts to open up north–south corridors which possibly bypass China and connect to the Indian subcontinent.

Fourth, in the long term China and the EU will seek to more aggressively secure their supply and value chains at transregional and intraregional levels. Both European and Chinese companies will try to create logistic redundancies by diversifying supply chains, keep full warehouses, partially repatriate production, or create independent production networks closer home – particularly in the chemical, pharmaceutical, and automotive sectors. Consequently, competition will increase over norms, standards, the control of new and emerging value and supply chains in critical new sectors like green energies, hydrogen, lithium-ion batteries, and digital technologies (AI), and critical infrastructure like power grids, telecommunications, ports, dry ports, terminals, and distribution. Geographic proximity will play a new relevant role in shortening supply chains and bringing production networks and final consumer markets closer together. For the EU, its immediate neighbourhood, starting with Eastern Europe but also including western Russia, the Caucasus, and potentially Central Asia, will gain further strategic relevance for the Union as European companies' supply and value chains may further shift eastward and southward from the current central European manufacturing core.

As a result, the relation between the EU and Russia might – but not necessarily will – evolve toward a more pragmatic and ad hoc form of cooperation, less than a strategic partnership but more than the current estrangement. To this presumable development will contribute not only China's rising political, economic, and technological influence but also the digitalization and regionalization of production and a green transition, as new low-carbon value and supply chains (hydrogen and e-cars) will require a redefinition of the traditional European–Russian gas and energy relation. Moscow for its part will not question the axis with Beijing; it will however be more willing to seek alternatives to China, making the Chinese–Russian partnership more fluid (Trenin, 2020).

For continental Eurasia, this will potentially open up chances for deeper institutional cooperation between the EAEU and the EU on trade, investments, production, and technology cooperation, especially considering that for the EU a complete re-shoring of production back to Europe or in its immediate periphery (nearshoring) will prove an illusion in the long term. Paradoxically, with the US's insulation, the EU will increasingly be called to balance domestic reshoring aspirations with the need for an even greater involvement in different regional Eurasian production networks. For the members of the Eurasian Economic Union to truly profit from this development, however, a substantial revision of the current relation between Russia and the EU will be needed. This, however, will not come without a difficult balancing act between the 'Chinese' and the 'European' vectors. Doubtless, a more fragmented world economy, based on fewer major regional economic blocs more or less fiercely sealed off from each other and increasingly independent from the West and Europe's technology, expertise, demand,

and production, might be a tempting argument for establishing an autarchic production, transport, and consumption space in continental Eurasia based on the EAEU. Considering the previously discussed structural weakness of Russia, the leading manufacturing and economic powerhouse in the Eurasian Economic Union, and the scarce interest of other members of the EAEU for such a model, COVID's long-term impact on the EU–China relation will presumably end up reinforcing the external orientation dilemma of continental Eurasia rather than fostering autarchic integration.

Conclusion
Geopolitical and geo-economic implications

The analysis of this book has shown that today, much like in the golden age of the early Eurasian 'globalized world system', the key to successful and sustainable integration of the transport space of continental Eurasia is less the ongoing expansion of transcontinental transit and more the participation in intraregional and transregional cross-border value chains. This is particularly true for the common economic and transport space of the EAEU, which represents the most advanced attempt to create a normative and regulatory unified framework for cross-border trade and transport across continental Eurasia since the collapse of the Soviet Union.

Without a doubt, the EAEU is only in its infancy and in the beginning of a long-term process, but it has already emerged as a reliable instrument to absorb external demand shocks by creating a regional market, particularly for Russian products. To date, however, this integration model has shown its limits, which might not be easy to overcome along with improved transport linkages. The creation of an integrated but autarchic transport and industrial space, potentially centred on Russia as the integration driver, has indeed proven problematic.

In fact, Moscow's low level of technological sophistication, industrial complexity, and financial firepower hampers further expansion of competitive value chains and direct investments, making the EAEU's attempt at greater transport integration only reasonable as an instrument for greater integration beyond the borders of the EAEU and of post-Soviet Eurasia.

On the contrary, the economic complementarities between continental Eurasia on one side and the two manufacturing blocs at the edges of the supercontinent, Europe and Asia, clearly represent the greatest asset for larger participation in global value chains via greater transport integration and logistic interoperability. This is even more true as the transformation in the geographic locations of economic activities and production networks, which has occurred within Europe (EU Enlargement) and China (Central and Western Development Strategy) throughout the past 15 years, has shortened the distance between Asian and European/German production networks and brought producers and consumers closer together across the continent.

This unprecedented transformation has given continental Eurasia, for the first time since the collapse of the Soviet Union, the chance to integrate into advanced value chains: since 2008, and particularly since the launch of the BRI in 2013, there has been increasing demand for transcontinental east–west (Asia–Europe) rail services across three main routes, two of which cross the entire territory of the EAEU. This has, for its part, certainly offered a grand incentive for establishing the Eurasian custom union – and later the EAEU – and for harmonizing tariffs across the Eurasian transport space.

These efforts have led to the creation of a more coordinated and functioning cross-border transport system, primarily among members of the EAEU (i.e., tariff harmonization, container-market liberalization, traction interoperability, joint rolling stock use, and coordination of integrated logistics services via the Unified Logistics Company). However, the development of transit corridors across this space presents limits, both in terms of few positive spillover effects on the development of intraregional domestic value and supply chains and in a lack of further integration into Europe's value chains – to date the biggest source of FDI and largest trade partner of continental Eurasia.

The latter is undoubtedly determined by the lack of a legal framework for deepening political–commercial cooperation between the EU and the EAEU as well as by a difficult political situation, chiefly the bilateral sanctions imposed by the EU and Russia because of the Ukraine crisis. This development has also accelerated continental Eurasia's opportunity to participate in the value and supply chains of the Asia Pacific, particularly with China. As mentioned, a blend of more institutionalized cooperation, a general and rapid reorientation of trade flows from Europe to Asia, and an increase in Chinese FDI in the non-oil and gas sectors – all catalyzed by China's BRI – are opening up concrete chances for greater Eurasian–Asian industrial and transport integration. However, this study has argued that under these circumstances, such reorientation might prove a long-term task with uncertain outcomes in the short to medium term.

In fact, a discussion of the potential and limitations of current east–west transport corridors, including relative to the integration of continental Eurasia within Asia's value chain, has shown that both transcontinental transit and regional industrial integration might exacerbate competition among continental Eurasian countries, including members of the EAEU. Competition might also not remain limited to the economic sphere; its implications could very well spill over into the geo-economic and geopolitical realm, with major consequences for continental Eurasia as a whole.

58 Conclusion

Today, greater (transport) connectivity, understood as the reterritorialization of the political economy of countries and regions via the reconfiguration of supply and value chains, production clusters, and demographic-urban concentration, is happening in the context of three major shifts, all accelerated by the COVID-19 pandemic outbreak of early 2020.

The first is a shift from globalization to fragmentation and the regionalization of supply and value chains, which is fuelled by technological changes like the Internet of Things and is influencing industrial production, energy generation, logistics, transport, and trade. The second is a shift from liberalization to the geo-politicization and weaponization of the economy. Rising technological, geopolitical, and normative competition is leading to greater stability risks, as power asymmetries and potential conflicts among emerging economic blocs can result in major disruptions of global value chains, supply routes, and trade and in more open forms of conflict, as shown by the US–Chinese trade war. The third is a shift from a transatlantic-centred liberal global order to a trans-Eurasian/transpacific system. Different, overlapping understandings of order but lacking 'shared rules' characterize this system, where political and economic pluralism is emerging besides and beyond the 'rise of China'. The shift from a transatlantic-centred to a Eurasian-Pacific-centred world is a long-term trend that can directly affect the nature of relations between major powers and blocs, specifically the United States, China, Europe, and Russia.

Against this backdrop, COVID has played a catalytic role in partially modifying and inserting new dynamic particularly in the EU–China relation. With both EU and China seeking to diversify their supply and value chains, secure access to a third market and control over new raw minerals supply chains, continental Eurasia, which borders all major power poles from Europe to the Indo-Pacific and Asia-Pacific regions, finds itself in the middle of contested but overlapping spheres of geo-economic influence.

Paramount for the impact of these developments is particularly the case of Russia, the driver of continental Eurasia's transport and economic integration and the major geopolitical player in this space.

Geopolitically, since Putin was re-elected president in 2012, Russia's political elites have essentially recognized the geopolitical potential and limits of Russia's pivot to Asia. With relations with Europe strained and the new axis with China full of unknown variables, Russia's turn to Asia has been matched by the launch of the EAEU and by its corollary concept of 'Greater Eurasia'. By establishing itself as the driving engine of continental Eurasian reintegration, Russia has sought to transform itself from an isolated periphery of Europe into a pivotal Euro-Eurasian power and to escape a dangerous unilateral dependence on Beijing. Geo-economically, however, strained relations with the West and Europe, together with Moscow's own economic weakness and need for expertise and technology transfer, exposes the limits of Russia's longitudinal geography and of its pivot to Asia/China. Amid COVID-19, while the Russia–Chinese relation has proven solid and even deepening, the nature of this relation has evolved toward greater asymmetry. With scarce alternatives in the West and a collapse in oil prices, Russia has found itself increasingly tightened in China's grip, particularly in terms of digital technologies and capital goods and as a final market for its energy resources. This has turned Russia's pivot to China from Russia's sovereign foreign policy decision into a necessity while narrowing space of manoeuvring.

Surely, the country's unique geographic extension makes Russia indispensable for a project like China's BRI initiative. However, Moscow seems to understand that for Russia to play a leading role in Asia, it will require more than a reorientation of oil and gas exports to the Pacific. Instead, the country needs an active policy of domestic economic and technological development that especially tackles the underdevelopment and isolation of its central and Far Eastern regions. For instance, even in case of a successfully accelerated modernization of the Far East but without proper coordination of a similar development strategy for Central Siberia, the former could eventually integrate into the Asia-Pacific space, leaving the latter isolated. In this case, Central Siberia, with a higher economic, industrial, and demographic base than the Far East but geographically isolated and disconnected from the Asia Pacific, would remain a landlocked periphery of Western Russia, serving as its primary industrial manufacturing base. The Far East would then turn into a raw material supplier for the advanced economies of the Asia Pacific once integrated with this macro-region.

However, the reconnection of Eurasia today is a phenomenon larger than a narrow 'post-Soviet' reintegration, only partially able to resolve Russian domestic imbalances along the east–west axis. As trade flows are shifting east and south along with new value and supply chains in Asia and Europe, the chance to create alternative overland and intermodal routes – and new value chains along different, more southerly routes – is increasing. In this context, China sees Russia as an important but not exclusive part of its project, with Beijing silently exploiting latent competition among transit countries to increase its political–economic leverage and gain the greatest possible flexibility. Therefore, if not carefully managed, China's drive for greater continental connectivity, augmented by the country's rapid recovery from the pandemic and foreseeable growing grip over continental digital and industrial value chains, might foster greater division more than greater integration among continental Eurasian countries. This could end up undermining Russia's attempt to exploit the BRI as an instrument to accelerate cross-regional integration under Moscow's leadership.

Conclusion

The Russian case shows particularly that the EAEU – thanks to the creation of a truly unified transport space – could indeed become the first step toward greater transport and industrial–political coordination across continental Eurasia at large, thus profiting from the BRI and from the increase in China's and Asia's FDI.

However, without serious domestic economic, industrial, and labour reforms; without the political willingness to accelerate cross-regional and intraregional transport and logistics integration inside the EAEU as well as coordination with other non-EAEU members; without diversifying trade and financial ties across Asia; and, finally, without normalizing the relations with the EU on a new basis, as a first step toward a more political–commercial dialogue, the geographical shift in Asia's and Europe's value chains as well as China's ambiguous and flexible transport politics might turn an unprecedented chance into a major risk. This fact could negatively affect transport integration across continental Eurasia by augmenting competition among and within countries over traffic volume, FDI, value chain participation, and ultimately geopolitical and geo-economic dividends.

Conversely, this study has shown that the COVID-19 pandemic-induced changes in the EU–China relation as well as the political and economic challenges faced by Beijing in Asia – set to accelerate the shift from China to South Asia and India as new engine of global growth – has also opened up unexpected chances for greater diversification, both in Asia and toward Europe.

While COVID has exposed continental Eurasia's dependence on China in economic, industrial, political, and infrastructural terms for the time being, in terms of transport corridors, the chances a post-COVID Eurasia might offer in the long term imply a major reorientation from exclusively east–west connections to intraregional north–south connections. From a geostrategic point of view, a major relevance will hence acquire new corridors like the International North-South Transport Corridor connecting the peripheral continental heartland with maritime Eurasia, the dynamic nexus stretching from the Baltic, Black, and Mediterranean Seas to the Indian and Pacific Oceans (Gresh, 2020).

To seize these opportunities and counterbalance the increased asymmetric dependence on China, however, continental Eurasia will need to more rapidly and decisively reach out to both Europe and other Asian countries like Japan, Korea, and India while more decisively implementing internal reforms for greater functional integration of its industries, markets, energy, and transport-logistic systems. The alternative would be geo-economic marginalization in both Europe and Asia and geopolitical insignificance.

References

Abe, D. (2020) 'Japan promises to diversify supply chains across ASEAN' *Nikkei Asia*, 20 October Available at: https://asia.nikkei.com/Politics/International-relations/Japan-promises-to-diversify-supply-chains-across-ASEAN (Accessed: 10 November 2020)

American Enterprise Institute (2020) 'China's investment tracker' Available at: www.aei.org/china-global-investment-tracker/ (Accessed: 20 November 2020)

ASEAN (2020a) 'ASEAN hits historic milestone with signing of RCEP' 15 November Available at: https://asean.org/asean-hits-historic-milestone-signing-rcep/ (Accessed: 19 November 2020)

ASEAN (2020b) 'Summary of the regional comprehensive economic partnership agreement' 15 November Available at: https://asean.org/storage/2020/11/Summary-of-the-RCEP-Agreement.pdf (Accessed: 19 November 2020)

ASEAN (2020c) 'Regional comprehensive economic partnership agreement-chapter 3-rules of origin' 15 November Available at: https://rcepsec.org/wp-content/uploads/2020/11/Chapter-3.pdf (Accessed: 22 November 2020)

Banning, T., and Mani, L. (2018) 'Iran-Europe transport corridors' *Eurailpress*, Volume 1 Available at: https://reconasia-production.s3.amazonaws.com/media/filer_public/89/e3/89e30271-19d7-459d-aedb-490b63a71ffd/irans_railway_dreams_-_tim_banning_article_v2.pdf (Accessed: 20 May 2020)

The Beijing Axis (2014) 'The China compass: Figures, forecast and analysis' Available at: http://www.thebeijingaxis.com/en/news-a-media/the-china-compass/107-the-china-compass-january-2014-1/file (Accessed: 13 June 2015)

Belarus News (2019a) 'Reorganization of Belarusian-Russian-Kazakh logistics company UTLC ERA over' 4 June Available at: https://eng.belta.by/economics/view/reorganization-of-belarusian-russian-kazakh-logistics-company-utlc-era-over-121574-2019/

Belarus News (2019b) 'Over 15,000 cars made by Belarusian-Chinese joint venture BelGee so far' 27 May Available at: https://eng.belta.by/economics/view/over-15000-cars-made-by-belarusian-chinese-joint-venture-belgee-so-far-121329-2019/

Berger, R. (2017) 'Eurasian rail corridors-What opportunities for stakeholders?' *International Union of Railways* Available at: https://uic.org/com/IMG/pdf/corridors_exe_sum2017_web.pdf

References

Buckley, P.J. (2020) 'China's belt and road initiative and the COVID-19 crisis' *Journal of International Business Policy*, Volume 3, pp. 311–314 Available at: https://doi.org/10.1057/s42214-020-00063-9 (Accessed: 17 November 2020)

Calder, K. (2011) *The new continentalism: Energy and 21st century geopolitics.* Yale University Press, New Haven, Connecticut.

Calder, K (2018) *Supercontinent. The logic of Eurasian integration.* Stanford University Press, Stanford, California.

Cerulus, L. (2020) 'Coronavirus forces Europe to confront China dependency-disruption across sectors amplifies calls in Europe and beyond to grow less reliant on China' *Politico*, 6 March Available at: www.politico.eu/article/coronavirus-emboldens-europes-supply-chain-security-hawks/ (Accessed: 10 October 2020)

Chang, G., Jiang, C., Chang, K., and Alam, B. (2013) 'Land prices and intracountry industrial relocation in China: Theory and the Yangtze Delta area case' *Chinese Economy*, Volume 46, No. 2, pp. 54–73

Daryl, G., and Sicong, X. (2020) 'Guide to China's dual circulation economy' *CGTN*, 25 October Available at: https://news.cgtn.com/news/2020-10-25/Guide-to-Chinas-dual-circulation-economy-US8jtau4h2/index.html (Accessed: 30 October 2020)

DB Cargo (2020) 'Current information covid-19: Currently no restrictions at DB Cargo Eurasia service' Available at: https://eurasia.dbcargo.com/2020/03/19/current-information-covid-19-currently-no-restrictions-at-db-cargo-eurasia-service/ (Accessed: 17 November 2020)

Economist Intelligence Unit (2020) 'The Great Unwinding: Covid-19 and the regionalisation of global supply chains' Available fro download at: https://www.eiu.com/n/campaigns/the-great-unwinding-covid-19-supply-chains-and-regional-blocs/ (Axccessed: 15 January 2021)

Eurasian Development Bank (2017) 'EAEU and Eurasia: Monitoring and analysis of direct investments' 21 December Available at: https://eabr.org/en/analytics/integration-research/cii-reports/eaeu-and-eurasia-monitoring-and-analysis-of-direct-investments-2017-/

Eurasian Development Bank (2019) 'Eurasian economic integration – Report 52' Available at: https://eabr.org/upload/iblock/211/EDB_Centre_Report_52_Eurasian_Economic_Integration_2019_eng.pdf

Eurasian Economic Commission (2014) 'Transport' Available at: www.eurasiancommission.org/ru/Documents/transport_eng.pdf (Accessed: 20 October 2020)

Eurasian Economic Commission (2016) 'Decision No. 133 of the council of the Eurasian economic commission' 21 December Available at: https://docs.eaeunion.org/docs/en-us/01414515/cncd_13012017_133 (Accessed: 20 September 2020)

Eurasian Economic Union (2014) 'Treaty on the Eurasian economic union' 5 June Available at: https://docs.eaeunion.org/docs/en-us/0027353/itia_05062014 (Accessed: 20 September 2020)

European Bank for Reconstruction and Development (2016) 'The EBRD's projects in the Russian railway sector' Available at: www.oecd.org/derec/ebrd/EBRD-EVD-Russian-rail-sector.pdf (Accessed: 25 September 2020)

European Commission (2020a) 'Countries and regions-China' 22 April Available at: https://ec.europa.eu/trade/policy/countries-and-regions/countries/china/ (Accessed: 18 November 2020)

References 63

European Commission (2020b) 'Countries and regions-Russia' 22 April Available at: https://ec.europa.eu/trade/policy/countries-and-regions/countries/russia/
European Commission (2020c) 'A new industrial strategy for Europe' 10 March Available at: https://ec.europa.eu/info/sites/info/files/communication-eu-industrial-strategy-march-2020_en.pdf (Accessed: 10 November 2020)
European Commission (2020d) 'A roadmap for recovery' 21 April Available at: www.consilium.europa.eu/media/43384/roadmap-for-recovery-final-21-04-2020.pdf (Accessed: 01 November 2020)
European Commission (2020e) 'Recovery plan for Europe' 10 November Available at: https://ec.europa.eu/info/strategy/recovery-plan-europe_en (Accessed: 11 November 2020)
European Commission (2020f) 'EU-Vietnam trade agreement enters into force' 30 July Available at: https://ec.europa.eu/commission/presscorner/detail/en/ip_20_1412 (Accessed: 30 August 2020)
European External Action Service (2020) 'Strengthening EU-ASEAN partnership, an urgent necessity – Statement by Joseph Borrell' 20 September Available at: https://eeas.europa.eu/headquarters/headquarters-homepage/85434/strengthening-eu-asean-partnership-urgent-necessity_en (Accessed: 20 October 2020)
European Union External Action Service (2018) 'Connecting Europe and Asia: Building blocks for an EU strategy' 19 September Available at: https://eeas.europa.eu/sites/eeas/files/joint_communication_-_connecting_europe_and_asia_-_building_blocks_for_an_eu_strategy_2018-09-19.pdf (Accessed: 25 September 2020)
Financial Tribune (2017) 'China finances Tehran-Isfahan high-speed railroad' *Financial Tribune*, 12 July Available at: https://financialtribune.com/articles/economy-domestic-economy/68698/china-finances-tehran-isfahanhigh-speed-railroad (Accessed: 28 September 2020)
Forbes (2020) 'Europe joins US companies moving out of China' 20 April Available at: https://forbes.ge/news/8338/Europe-Joins-US-Companies-Moving-Out-Of-China (Accessed: 20 November 2020)
Gabuev, A. (2020) 'The pandemic could tighten China's grip on Eurasia' *Foreign Policy*, 23 April Available at: https://foreignpolicy.com/2020/04/23/coronavirus-pandemic-china-eurasia-russia-influence/ (Accessed: 20 October 2020)
Gakuto, T. (2020) 'RCEP to remove tariffs on 86% of Japan's exports to China' *Nikkei Asia*, 15 November Available at: https://asia.nikkei.com/Politics/International-relations/RCEP-to-remove-tariffs-on-86-of-Japan-s-exports-to-China (Accessed: 17 November 2020)
Garcia-Herrero, A. (2020) 'RCEP might not stop reshuffling of Asian value chains' *Asia Times*, 17 November Available at: https://asiatimes.com/2020/11/rcep-might-not-stop-reshuffling-of-asian-value-chains/ (Accessed: 22 November 2020)
Gerden, E. (2018) 'Russia rail aims for Asia imports to South and Central Europe' *Journal of Commerce*, 4 September Available at: www.joc.com/rail-intermodal/russia-rail-aim-asia-imports-south-and-central-europe_20180904.html (Accessed: 17 November 2020)
German Chamber of Commerce in China (2018) 'Labour market and salary report 2018/2019' Available at: https://china.ahk.de/fileadmin/AHK_China/Market_Info/Economic_Data/GCC-11th-Labor-Market-and-Salary-Report-2018_short.pdf (Accessed: 17 November 2020)

References

German Federal Ministry for Economy and Energy, French Ministry of Economy and Finances (2019) 'Franco-German manifesto for a European industrial policy' Available at: www.bmwi.de/Redaktion/DE/Downloads/F/franco-german-manifesto-for-a-european-industrial-policy.pdf?__blob=publicationFile&v=2 (Accessed: 10 November 2020)

German Federal Statistics Office (2019) 'Die Volksrepublik China ist erneut deutschlands wichtigster handelspartner' Available at: www.destatis.de/DE/Themen/Wirtschaft/Aussenhandel/handelspartner-jahr.html (Accessed: 17 November 2020)

Gresh, G.F. (2020) *To rule Eurasia's waves: The new great power competition at sea*. Yale University Press, New Haven, Connecticut.

Hale, T. (2020) 'China's export growth hits highest level in 19 months' *Financial Times*, 7 November Available at: www.ft.com/content/ddc54582-ffa0-4d25-b3a9-0b8e87a894ad (Accessed: 12 November 2020)

Handelsblatt (2018) 'Wegen US-sanktionen: Siemens will geschäfte im Iran zurückfahren' *Handelsblatt*, 24 August Available at: www.handelsblatt.com/unternehmen/industrie/wegen-us-sanktionen-siemens-will-geschaefte-im-iran-zurueckfahren/22949178.html?ticket=ST-3999988-GvjsY3SPOCqefYeDJHWV-ap6 (Accessed: 12 November 2020)

Handelszeitung (2018) 'Stadler liegt milliardenauftrag mit Iran auf Eis' *Handelszeitung*, 8 August Available at: www.handelszeitung.ch/unternehmen/stadler-legt-milliardenauftrag-im-iran-auf-eis (Accessed: 18 November 2020)

Hürriyet Daily News (2019) 'China railway express crosses Europe via Marmaray' *Hürriyet Daily News*, 6 November Available at: www.hurriyetdailynews.com/china-railway-express-crosses-europe-via-marmaray-148384 (Accessed: 18 November 2020)

International Transport Forum (2019) *Enhancing connectivity and freight in central Asia*. OECD Available at: www.itf-oecd.org/sites/default/files/docs/connectivity-freight-central-asia_2.pdf (Accessed: 17 November 2020)

Jakobowski, J., Poplawski, K., and Kaczmarski, M. (2018) 'The EU-China rail connections: Background, actors, interests' *Center for Eastern Studies* Available at: www.osw.waw.pl/sites/default/files/studies_72_silk-railroad_net.pdf (Accessed: 20 November 2020)

Kaplan, R.D. (2017) *The return of Marco Polo's world and the US military response*. Center for a New American Security. Washington, D.C.

Knowler, G (2017) Hutchison UK: Asia-Europe rail won't dent ocean volume Journal of Commerce 14 September 2017, https://www.joc.com/rail-intermodal/booming-asia-europe-rail-trade-won%E2%80%99t-dent-ocean-volume-says-hutchison-uk-head_20170914.html (Accessed: 14 January 2021)

Knowler, G. (2018) 'Huge subsidies keep China-Europe rail network on track' *Journal of Commerce*, 23 May Available at: www.joc.com/rail-intermodal/huge-subsidies-keep-china-europe-rail-network-track_20180523.html (Accessed: 25 August 2020)

Kofner, Y. (2019) 'Ten reasons for EU–EAEU cooperation' *Valdai Club*, 26 June Available at: https://valdaiclub.com/a/highlights/ten-reasons-for-eaeu-eu-cooperation/ (Accessed: 17 November 2020)

Kofner, Y. (2020a) 'EAEU industrial cooperation: Promising products with intra-union demand' *Institute for Market Integration and Economic Policy*, 20 April Available at: https://miwi-institut.de/archives/426?fbclid=IwAR1__O_CIVPqqm-

References

b8u3CRWpj8Dc5bBI6vVMRx2adnLKBwmuCurVuVlPaxZI (Accessed: 17 October 2020)

Kofner, Y. (2020b) 'Potential trade and welfare effects of trade liberalization between China and the Eurasian economic union' *Institute for Market Integration and Economic Policy*, 16 June Available at: https://miwi-institut.de/archives/635 (Accessed: 25 October 2020)

Koty, A.C. (2019) 'Disparities in China's regional growth: A look at H1 2019 GDP data' *China Briefing*, 9 September Available at: www.china-briefing.com/news/china-regional-growth-disparities-increased-h1-2019-gdp-growth-numbers/ (Accessed: 15 October 2020)

Koty, A.C. (2020) 'What is the China standards 2035 plan and how will it impact emerging industries' *ChinaBriefing*, 2 July Available at: www.china-briefing.com/news/what-is-china-standards-2035-plan-how-will-it-impact-emerging-technologies-what-is-link-made-in-china-2025-goals/ (Accessed: 20 July 2020)

Lall, S.V., and Lebrand, M. (2019) 'Who wins, who loses? Understanding the spatially differentiated effects of the Belt and Road Initiative' *The World Bank* Available at: http://documents.worldbank.org/curated/en/292161554727963020/pdf/Who-Wins-Who-Loses-Understanding-the-Spatially-Differentiated-Effects-of-the-Belt-and-Road-Initiative.pdf (Accessed: 15 July 2020)

Lobyrev, V., Tikhomirov, A., Tsukarev, T., and Vinokurov, E. (2018) 'Belt and road transport corridors: Barriers and investments' *MPRA Paper No. 86705*, 18 May Available at: https://mpra.ub.uni-muenchen.de/86705/1/MPRA_paper_86705.pdf (Accessed: 15 July 2020)

National Development and Reform Commission (2016) 'China railway express 2016–2020' Available at: http://www.ndrc.gov.cn/zcfb/zcfbghwb/201610/P020161017547345656182.pdf

Noack, R. (2018) 'China's new train line to Iran sends message to Trump: We'll keep trading anyway' *Washington Post*, 11 May Available at: www.washingtonpost.com/news/world/wp/2018/05/11/chinas-new-train-line-to-iran-sends-message-to-trump-well-keep-trading-anyway/?noredirect=on&utm_term=.e0b04b60aef0 (Accessed: 15 July 2020)

Noerr (2016) 'Russia facilitation of rules on industrial assembly agreements' 4 December Available at: www.noerr.com/en/newsroom/News/russia-facilitation-of-rules-on-industrial-assembly-agreements (Accessed: 20 November 2020)

OECD (2019) 'Global material resources outlook to 2060 economic drivers and environmental consequences' Available at: https://espas.secure.europarl.europa.eu/orbis/sites/default/files/generated/document/en/OECD.pdf (Accessed: 10 November 2020)

OECD (2020) 'Building confidence amid an uncertain recovery-OECD interim report September 2020' OECD Available at: www.oecd.org/economic-outlook/ (Accessed: 18 November 2020)

Pak, E. (2016) 'Rethinking common transport and logistics policy of the Eurasian economic union' *Review of Economic Studies and Research*, Volume 7, No. 3 Available at: http://eurasian-studies.org/archives/2689 (Accessed: 18 November 2011)

Pepe, J.M. (2017) *Continental drift: Germany and China's inroads in the 'German central Eastern European manufacturing core': Geopolitical chances and risks*. Johns Hopkins University School of Advanced International Studies, Washington, D.C.

References

Pepe, J.M. (2018) *Beyond energy: Trade and transport in a reconnecting Eurasia.* Springer Verlag, Wiesbaden.

Pepe, J.M. (2019) 'The "Eastern polygon" of the trans-Siberian rail line: A critical factor for assessing Russia's strategy toward Eurasia and the Asia-Pacific' *Asia Europe Journal*, pp. 1–20 Available at: https://doi.org/10.1007/s10308-019-00543-5 (Accessed: 18 November 2020)

Petri, P.A., and Plummer, M. (2020) 'China could help stop the freefall in global economic cooperation' *Brookings Blog*, 16 July Available at: www.brookings.edu/blog/order-from-chaos/2020/07/16/china-could-help-stop-the-freefall-in-global-economic-cooperation/?fbclid=IwAR1zTer4vGQ5P34kIppXBS7vPcOkpfU998UuWwHBSjbnuxoBllK6cL5UezY (Accessed: 22 November 2020)

Pomfret, R. (2018) 'The Eurasian land bridge: Linking regional value chains' *Voxeu*, 1 May Available at: https://voxeu.org/article/eurasian-landbridge-linking-regional-value-chains (Accessed: 18 November 2020).

Pomfret, R. (2020) *China's belt and road initiative, the Eurasian Land Bridge, and the new mega-regionalism.* World Scientific Press, Singapore.

Railway Gazette International (2017) 'Teheran – Mashhad electrification loan signed' *Railway Gazette International*, 25 July Available at: www.railwaygazette.com/news/infrastructure/single-view/view/tehran-mashhad-electrification-loan-signed.html (Accessed: 20 November 2020)

Rastogi, C., and Arvis, J.F. (2014) *The Eurasian connection: Supply-chain efficiency along the modern silk route through central Asia.* The World Bank, Washington, D.C.

Reynolds, I., and Urabe, E. (2020) 'Japan to fund firms to shift production out of China' *Bloomberg*, 8 April Available at: www.bloomberg.com/news/articles/2020-04-08/japan-to-fund-firms-to-shift-production-out-of-china (Accessed: 17 November 2020)

Rhodium Group (2020) 'Chinese FDI in Europe 2019' Available at: https://rhg.com/research/chinese-fdi-in-europe-2019-update/#:~:text=The%20analysis%20shows%20that%20Chinese,levels%20(EUR%2017.4%20billion (Accessed: 17 November 2020)

Rogers, D. (2015) 'Iran's railway revolution' *Global Construction Review*, 14 December Available at: www.globalconstructionreview.com/markets/how-islamic-republic-set-become-land-br8i8d8ge/ (Accessed: 18 November 2020)

Shilina, M. (2019) 'Analysis of EAEU–China agreement on economic and trade cooperation' 26 January https://doi.org/10.3390/economies7040118

Sohrabi, Z. (2018) 'Three freight trains due in Tehran from China this week' *Financial Tribune*, 9 January Available at: https://financialtribune.com/articles/domestic-economy/79577/three-freight-trains-due-in-tehran-fromchina-this-week (Accessed: 18 November 2020)

Stehrer, R., and Stöllinger, R. (2015) 'The central European manufacturing core: What is driving regional production sharing?' *FIW-Research Reports 2014/15 N° 02* Available at: www.fiw.ac.at/fileadmin/Documents/Publikationen/Studien_2014/Studien_2014_adapted_file_names_stoellinger/02_Stoellinger_FIW_Research_Report_The_Central_European_Manufacturing_Core_What_is_Driving_Regional_Production_Sharing.pdf (Accessed: 18 November 2020)

References

Suk-yee, J. (2020) 'South Korean government to promote reshoring' *Business Korea*, 2 June Available at: www.businesskorea.co.kr/news/articleView.html?idxno=46788 (Accessed: 20 November 2020)

Trenin, D. (2020) 'How Russia can maintain equilibrium in the post-pandemic bipolar world' *Carnegie Moscow Center*, 1 May Available at: https://carnegie.ru/commentary/81702 (Accessed: 6 November 2020)

Tsurkov, M. (2018) 'A historic year for Azerbaijan's transport sector' *Azernews*, 2 January Available at: www.azernews.az/news_print.php?news_id=124903 2/3 (Accessed: 20 November 2020)

Ustyuzhanina, E. (2016) 'The Eurasian union and global value chains' *European Politics and Society*, Volume 17 (s1), pp. 35–45

Vakulchuk, R., Øverland, I., Aminjonov, F., Abylkasymova, A., Eshchanov, B., and Moldokanov, D. (2019) 'BRI in central Asia: Overview of Chinese projects' *Central Asia Data-Gathering and Analysis Team (CADGAT)* Available at: www.researchgate.net/publication/333673045 (Accessed: 20 November 2020)

van Leijen, M. (2018) 'Malzewice-Brest border crossing main bottleneck on new silk road' *RailFreight*, 29 March Available at: www.railtech.com/infrastructure/2018/03/29/malzewicze-brest-border-crossing-main-bottleneck-on-new-silk-road/ (Accessed: 20 November 2020)

van Leijen, M. (2019) 'Chinese subsidies for the New Silk Road on a decline' *RailFreight*, 1 October Available at: www.railfreight.com/specials/2019/10/01/chinese-subsidies-for-the-new-silk-road-on-a-decline/ (Accessed: 20 November 2020)

van Leijen, M. (2020a) 'Monthly traffic China-Europe exceeds 52k TEUs for first time' *Railfreight*, 9 July Available at: www.railfreight.com/beltandroad/2020/07/09/monthly-traffic-china-europe-exceeds-52k-teus-for-first-time/ (Accessed: 17 November 2020)

van Leijen, M. (2020b) 'New records set on the middle corridor to Turkey' *Railfreight*, 6 July Available at: www.railfreight.com/beltandroad/2020/07/06/new-records-set-on-the-middle-corridor-to-turkey/ (Accessed: 17 November 2020)

Veliyev, C. (2020) 'COVID-19 increases importance of middle corridor' *Eurasia Daily Monitor*, Volume 15, No. 17 Available at: https://jamestown.org/program/covid-19-increases-importance-of-middle-corridor/ (Accessed: 15 November 2020)

Verband Deutscher Maschinen-und Anlagenbau (2018) 'Neue VDMA China-Studie Das Chinageschäft der Zukunft – Herausforderungen und Strategien für den deutschen Maschinenbau' 15 October Available at: www.vdma.org/article/-/articleview/12174612 https://aussenwirtschaft.vdma.org/viewer/-/v2article/render/26925288 (Accessed: 25 November 2020)

Vinokurov, E. (2018) *Introduction to the Eurasian economic union*. London: Palgrave Macmillan

Wan, Z., and Liu, X. (2009) 'Chinese railway transportation: Opportunity and challenge' Available at: https://pdfs.semanticscholar.org/13d2/fa2f8433ddf01258c62f5cf0b79bbddb6b3d.pdf?_ga=2.106219655.528118586.1576681578-888137524.1576681578

References

Westwood, J.N. (2002) *Soviet railways to Russian railways*. Palgrave Macmillan, London.

The World Bank (2018a) 'International logistics performance index' Available at: https://lpi.worldbank.org/international (Accessed: 20 November 2020)

The World Bank (2018b) 'Aggregated logistics performance index' Available at: https://lpi.worldbank.org/international/aggregated-ranking (Accessed: 20 November 2020)

The World Bank (2018c) 'Logistics performance index: Global rankings 2018' Available at: https://lpi.worldbank.org/international/global/2018 (Accessed: 20 November 2020)

Xinhua (2017) 'Full text: List of deliverables of belt and road forum' 15 May Available at: http://news.xinhuanet.com/english/2017-05/15/c_136286376.htm (Accessed: 25 November 2020)

Ziyadov, T. (2012) *Azerbaijan as a regional hub in central Eurasia. Strategic assessment of Euro-Asian trade and transportation*. Baku: ADA-Azerbaijan Diplomatic Academy Press

Index

Note: Page numbers in *italic* indicate a figure on the corresponding page.

Africa, trade with 36–37
agriculture and food processing industry 39
Aktau port, Kazakhstan 28–30
Alyat port, on Caspian Sea 29
Anaklia port, Georgia 29
Armenia: rail lines 9
ASEAN 50–52
Asia: free trade agreement 50–52; trade with 36–37
Australia: ASEAN free trade agreement 50
automotive markets 16, 39
Azerbaijan: in Middle Corridor 29–30
Azerbaijan Caspian Shipping Company CJSC 29

Baku–Tiflis–Kars (BTK) railway 29
Baltic Railway Branch 9
Belarus: bottleneck in Northern Corridor 25–26; Chinese FDI 39
Belt and Road Initiative (BRI) 2, 5; effect of COVID-19 48–50, 52; geo-economic implications 59–60; role in east–west rail transport corridors 19–24, *25*
Black Sea, in Middle Corridor 29

cargo tons *see* freight volume
Caspian Sea, in Middle Corridor 28–29, 45
Central Asian Railway 9
Chengdu, China 17, 18, 24, 27, 31, 41

China: Asian free trade agreement 50–52; BRI *see* Belt and Road Initiative (BRI); Central and Western Development Strategy 3, 17, 56; COVID-19 and Eurasian transport integration 54–55; diversification of value chains 38–39, 58; dual economic circulation doctrine 5, 50–52; EAEU non-preferential trade agreement 38, 39–40; EAEU subsidies 20, 22–23; economic growth 49; EU overreliance on 46–48; first freight train 29–30; five-year railway plan 26–27; foreign direct investment (FDI) 37–40, 49, 53; manufacturing and production hubs 17–18, 26–27, 34; Middle Corridor 28–30; Northern Corridor 24–28, 30; Southern Corridor 31–32; trade conflict with US 37, 45–46, 47, 58; trade with Eurasia 4, 5, 35–37, 40–43; trade with Europe 2, 16–17, 20; value chains go west 17–18
Chongqing, China 17, 18, 19, 24, 27, 31, 41
Commonwealth of Independent States (CIS) 38
Constanta Port 29
continental Eurasia: defined 7n1
continentalization of value chains: China goes west 17–18; Europe goes east 15–17

70   *Index*

corridors for transport: International North-South Transport Corridor 60; *see also* east–west transit corridors
COVID-19 pandemic 44–55; China's dual circulation and free trade agreement with Asia 48–52; effect on supply chains 5; EU overreliance on China and strategic autonomy 46–48; Eurasia's transport integration 52–55; geopolitical and geo-economic implications 58–60; as trend accelerator 44–46
cross-regional value chains, history of 1–4

Deutsche Bahn 19, 22
digital technologies (5G) 47, 48, 52
dual economic circulation doctrine 5, 50–52

EAEU (Eurasian Economic Union): creation of 4, 10; defined 7n1; geopolitical and geo-economic implications 56–60; non-preferential trade agreement with China 38, 39–40; trade, mutual and external 12–13; transport integration 10–12, 19–20, 40–43, 54–55
Eastern Siberia–Pacific Ocean oil pipeline 2
east–west transit corridors 19–33, 34, 57; BRI's role in 19–24, *25*; Middle Corridor 28–30; Northern Corridor 24–28; Southern Corridor 30–33
Eurasia: defined 7n1; economic models of countries 2–4; transport integration in continent 8–14, 40–43, 52–55
Eurasian–Asian trade: rise of 35–37
Eurasian Custom Union 4, 57
Eurasian Economic Commission 11
Eurasian Economic Union *see* EAEU (Eurasian Economic Union)
Europe/European Union (EU): COVID-19 and Eurasian transport integration 54–55; foreign direct investment (FDI) 38; free trade agreement with Vietnam 51; overreliance on China and strategic autonomy 46–48, 49; trade with China 2, 16–17, 20; value chains go east 15–17

foreign direct investment (FDI) 37–40, 49, 53
freight volume 23, 29, 31, 36–37
French-German Industrial Policy Manifesto 47

gas pipelines 2; *see also* oil and gas industry
geopolitical and geo-economic implications 56–60
Georgia: Black Sea ports 29–30; rail lines 9
German–Central-Eastern European Manufacturing Core (GCEMC) 15–17
Germany: French-German Industrial Policy Manifesto 47
global value chains (GVC) 3, 17, 46
green initiatives 48, 52, 54

history of transport and trade in Eurasia 1–4
Horgos, China 17, 27

India: RCEP free trade agreement 51–52; trade with China 46
Indian Ocean freight routes 36–37; *see also* seaborne trade
infrastructure: China's support of 18, 31; in Northern Corridor 25–26; in Southern Corridor 31–32
Inner Mongolia 27, 31
International North-South Transport Corridor 60
Iran: closed borders 45; Southern Corridor 30–33

Japan: ASEAN free trade agreement 50–52
just-in-time delivery 19, 22

Kashgar, China 17, 31
Kazakhstan: Northern Corridor 24–28; rail network 9; transport integration between Russia and China 41–42, 43
Kazakhstan Railways JSC 29
Korea: ASEAN free trade agreement 50–52

Lianyungang port, China 24, 42, 43

manufacturing: Europe's core 3,
15–17; production hubs in China
17–18, 26–27, 34; trade in EAEU
12–13
maritime Eurasian countries:
defined 7n1
Mediterranean/Caspian freight routes 37
metals and mineral products: trade in
EAEU 12–13
Middle Corridor 28–30, 43, 45

New Eurasian Land Bridge 24, 42, 43
New Zealand: ASEAN free trade
agreement 50
Next Generation EU 48
Northern Corridor 24–28
Novorossiysk 29

OECD in global GDP 46
oil and gas industry 2, 38–39, 40

pipelines, oil and gas 2
Poland: bottleneck in Northern
Corridor 25–26
political issues: between EU and EAEU
38; between US and China 45–46;
geopolitical implications 56–60;
instability in Middle East 32
Power of Siberia gas pipeline 2

rail cargo transport: China's five-year
plan 26–27; electrification 31; gauge
changes 30, 31; shipping costs
21–22; unloading times of container
trains 25–26, 30
rail ferry, Lake Van 32
rail lines: Asia–Europe cargo transport
see east–west transit corridors;
transport integration and 8
Recovery and Resilience Facility
(rescEU) 48
Regional Comprehensive Economic
Partnership (RCEP) 41, 50–51, 53
roads in continental Eurasia 8; see also
rail lines
Russia: COVID-19 and Eurasian
transport integration 54–55; Far East
development 42, 59; foreign direct
investment (FDI) 38; geopolitical
implications 56–60; industrial policy
11; Northern Corridor 24–28; rail

network 8–10; Siberian integration
42, 59; transport integration between
Kazakhstan and China 41–42; see
also Trans-Siberian rail line

seaborne trade 2, 20–21, 36–37
Southeast Asia: Chinese FDI in 53; as
future engine of global growth 45, 46
Southern Corridor 30–33, 43
Southern Silk Road 30
Soviet Ministry of Railways 9
Soviet Union: history of value and
supply chains 1–2; rail network
8–9, 10
special economic zones 17, 41

Tajikistan: rail line 10
Teheran 31
TEU (20-foot equivalent unit) 2, 20
time and timeliness, in rail cargo
transport 23–24
trade ties between Asia and Eurasia
34–43; Asian FDI in continental
Eurasia 37–40; Eurasia's transport
integration in Asia's value and supply
chains 40–43; rise of trade 35–37
Trans-Caucasian Railway 9
transit corridors for transport see
corridors for transport
transit royalties 34
Transport Corridor Europe–Caucasus–
Asia (TRACECA) 28–29
transport integration in continental
Eurasia 8–14, 40–43, 52–55
Trans-Siberian rail line 8, 10, 24, 26, 42
Trans-Siberian–Trans-Mongolian
route 42
Turkey: east–west rail network 30, 32;
Southern Corridor 30–33
Turkmenbashi port, Turkmenistan
28–29
Turkmen–Iranian–Turkish route 45
Turkmen Railway 9

Ukraine crisis 38, 57
Unified Logistics Company 57
United States: trade conflicts 37,
45–46, 47, 58
United Transport and Logistics
Company–Eurasian Rail Alliance 12
urbanization 10, 41

Urumqi, China 17, 31
Uzbekistan: rail lines 9–10

V4 countries: regional production network 15–17
value chains: diversification by China 38–39, 58; global (GVC) 3, 17, 46; history of cross-regional 1–4; *see also* continentalization of value chains
Vietnam: free trade agreement with EU 51

Zhongyuan, China 17, 18